Peace Pilgrim

Peace
Pilgrim

HER LIFE AND WORK
IN HER OWN WORDS

Compiled by some of her friends.

AN   OCEAN   TREE   BOOK

Santa Fe, New Mexico   •   1991

Also by Peace Pilgrim —
   STEPS TOWARD INNER PEACE (in English, Spanish and Russian)
This little booklet is available free of charge, as it was for many years during Peace's
pilgrimage. For this booklet, as well as audio and video tapes of Peace Pilgrim speaking
and other materials about Peace Pilgrim, write to:
   Friends of Peace Pilgrim
            Telephone (909) 927-7678
   43480 Cedar Avenue, Hemet, CA 92544

An Ocean Tree Book
   Post Office Box 1295
   Santa Fe, New Mexico 87504
Write to Ocean Tree Books for a list of related titles.

Printed in the United States of America
   First printing: December 1982   Compact Edition: August 1988
   Tenth printing: January 1991   Hardcover Edition: Spring 1991

Designed by Richard Polese with Patricia Yohn
Cover photograph by Jim Burton, *Topeka Capital-Journal*

International Standard Book Numbers:
   0-943734-01-0 (standard paperbound)
   0-943734-15-0 (compact edition)
   0-943734-20-7 (hardcover edition)

Library of Congress Cataloging in Publication Data:

Peace Pilgrim, d. 1981.
   Peace Pilgrim: her life and work in her own words.
   1. Peace Pilgrim, d. 1981. 2. Pacifists—United States—Biography.
I. Title.
JX1962.P35A36 1982   327.1'72'0924 [B]   82-18854
ISBN 0-943734-15-0

Lovingly dedicated to all seekers.

photograph by Carla Anette

*I am a pilgrim, a wanderer. I shall remain a wanderer until
mankind has learned the way of peace, walking until I am given shelter
and fasting until I am given food.*

—Peace Pilgrim

Introducing Peace Pilgrim

YOU MAY SEE HER walking through your town or along the highway — a silver-haired woman dressed in navy blue slacks and shirt, and a short tunic with pockets all around the bottom in which she carries her only worldly possessions. It says "PEACE PILGRIM" in white letters on the front of the tunic and "25,000 Miles On Foot for Peace" on the back. She has walked the 25,000 miles. However, she continues to walk, for her vow is, "I shall remain a wanderer until mankind has learned the way of peace, walking until I am given shelter and fasting until I am given food." She walks without a penny in her pockets and she is not affiliated with any organization. She walks as a prayer and as a chance to inspire others to pray and work with her for peace. She speaks to individuals along the way, to gatherings such as church groups or college groups, through newspapers, magazines, radio, television — relating interesting and meaningful experiences, discussing peace within and without. She feels we have learned that war is not the way to peace — that security does not lie in stockpiles of bombs. She points out that this is a crisis period in human history, and that we who live in the world today must choose between a nuclear war of annihilation and a golden age of peace. Although she does not ask to see results, thousands of letters testify that her journey has not been in vain — saying, in effect, "Since talking with you I've decided that I should be doing something for peace also."

(This message was printed on a brief leaflet, a few copies of which Peace Pilgrim carried in her tunic in order to introduce herself.)

Contents

Appendices

Introduction

PEACE PILGRIM had an impact on people as she walked joyfully across the country that will never be adequately expressed. She awakened and inspired many thousands during her twenty-eight year pilgrimage for peace. Those she touched in a personal way carry very special memories — talking, laughing, walking together; listening to pilgrimage stories over the dinner table or while driving her to a speaking engagement; waving goodbyes as she quickly departed for her next destination.

From 1953 until 1981 this silver-haired woman, with cheerful obedience to her calling, was a server in the world. As she approached each country hamlet or sprawling city she carried to all she met a message of peace expressed so simply: When enough of us find *inner peace,* our institutions will become more peaceful and there will be no more occasion for war.

Following her death in 1981, a number of her friends from throughout the country gathered in Santa Fe, New Mexico, to remember her and share our experiences of her. A small group stayed on to work on the book project, an idea which had been in our hearts individually for some time. We have attempted in this book to present Peace Pilgrim's extraordinary life and teachings in their purest form — her own words. They were assembled from her little booklet, *Steps Toward Inner Peace,* her nineteen *Peace Pilgrim's Progress* newsletters, private conversations, excerpts from her correspondence and talks taped by many individuals over the years. Other valuable resources were the thousands of newspaper articles and other printed material in the Peace Pilgrim Collection of the Swarthmore College Peace Library.

Although the words are her own, this book was not written by her as an autobiography. Some material was transcribed verbatim from tapes, which gives certain passages a spoken rather than a written quality. We wish she had written her own book. People often asked if she would write her own story, and more than once

she answered, "I have really written enough material for a book —
it's just not in book form."

Putting it into book form has been our job.

Though her basic message never changed, variety of detail and
experience color each of her communications. You may find
several of her concise statements of principles or aphorisms
repeated, but usually in a new context.

ℐ

The simple yet profound message of Peace Pilgrim's life and
words is urgently needed in humankind's search for peace. She has
given us renewed hope in the future of this world — hope that
enough might gain inner peace to make world peace possible. She
has given us an example of a person who *lived* in inner peace and
was filled with a boundless energy that grew rather than
diminished with age.

Robert Steele wrote in the Indian journal *Gandhi Marg*: "Peace
Pilgrim speaks with astonishing authority and confidence; she
reminds one of the spokesmen of God of biblical times. However,
her utterances do not sound like a fanatic or dogmatist. Instead,
they sound like a deeply sincere and devoted human being who has
been linked to a wise and ineffable vision..."

Known from coast to coast simply as Peace Pilgrim, it was her
wish to stress "the message and not the messenger." She never
told details of her life that she considered unimportant, such as her
original name, age, and birthplace. Since this book is about her
pilgrimage in her own words, we have decided not to include these
specifics, which can be found elsewhere.

"I never want people to remember me except in connection
with peace," she said. To those of us who knew her well and saw
her over a number of years she will always remain the serene,
warm-hearted Peace Pilgrim — full of humor, vitality and the joy
of living.

Born on a small farm in the East in the early part of this
century, she grew from modest roots and, like many people,
gradually acquired money and things. When she realized this self-
centered life had become meaningless, and worldly goods burdens
to her rather than blessings, she walked all one night through the

woods until she felt "a complete willingness, without any reservations, to give my life to God and to service."

She gradually and methodically adopted a life of voluntary simplicity. She began what was to be a fifteen-year period of preparation, not knowing just what it was she was preparing for. She did volunteer work for peace groups and also worked with people who had physical, emotional and mental problems.

During this 'preparation period' and in the midst of many spiritual hills and valleys, she found inner peace — and her calling.

Her pilgrimage for peace began on the morning of January 1, 1953. She vowed "to remain a wanderer until mankind has learned the way of peace." Peace Pilgrim walked alone and penniless and with no organizational backing. She walked "as a prayer" and as a chance to inspire others to pray and work for peace. She wore navy blue shirt and slacks, and a short tunic with pockets all around the bottom in which she carried her only worldly possessions: a comb, a folding toothbrush, a ballpoint pen, copies of her message and her current correspondence.

After walking 25,000 miles, which took until 1964, she stopped counting miles and speaking became her first priority, although she continued to walk daily. Her increasing speaking schedule made it necessary for her to begin to accept rides often.

Peace Pilgrim talked with thousands of people throughout the McCarthy era, the Korean war, the Vietnam war and since. She met with people on city streets and dusty roads, in ghettos, suburbs, deserts and truckstops. She was interviewed by all national radio and TV networks, as well as on hundreds of local stations across the country. Newspaper reporters in countless towns and cities large and small wrote about her. She would seek them out, if they didn't find her first, to let people hear about her message. She talked to university classes in psychology, political science, philosophy and sociology, to high school assemblies, civic clubs, and spoke from the pulpits of a variety of churches.

As the years went by, her contagious zest, ready wit and simple wisdom widened her appeal, and audiences responded more and more frequently with warm and spontaneous laughter and thoughtful questions.

And all of these years when many of us were increasingly afraid to go out on our streets, she walked through 'dangerous' parts of cities and slept beside the road, on beaches and in bus stations, when no bed was offered. Through the years strangers became friends, inviting her into their homes and arranging speaking engagements, often a year or more in advance.

Peace Pilgrim believed we had entered a crisis period in human history, "walking the brink between a nuclear war of annihilation and a golden age of peace." She felt it was her calling to arouse people from apathy and get them thinking and actively working for peace. And always she encouraged people to seek the real source of peace within, and to use the ways of peace in their relations with others.

♫

At the time of her death Peace Pilgrim was crossing the country for the seventh time. She had walked through all fifty states, and had also visited the ten provinces in Canada and parts of Mexico. In 1976 a man flew her to Alaska and Hawaii to meet his children, walk, speak in churches, and talk with the media. In 1979 and 1980 she returned to those states, taking with her small groups of people who wished to learn more about her lifestyle. She had plans for return trips to Alaska and Hawaii in 1984 and was giving thought to inviting others to join her on 'inspirational tours' through several states in the years that were to come.

She made what she liked to call "the glorious transition to a freer life" on July 7, 1981 near Knox, Indiana. She died instantly in a head-on collision as she was being driven to a speaking engagement. Her many friends throughout the country were stunned. Somehow, we never imagined Peace would be called to leave this earth life so soon. Yet, one friend wrote, "I feel sure the immediacy of the transition, with no cessation of her activity until it occurred, was as she would have wished it."

In her last newspaper interview she spoke of being in radiant health. She was planning her itinerary beyond the current pilgrimage route and had speaking engagements through 1984. Ted Hayes of WKVI radio in Knox in an interview with her taped on July 6 remarked, "You seem to be a most happy woman." She replied, "I certainly *am* a happy person. How could one know God and not be joyous?"

Messages from friends who hear of her passing continue to be received at the little Cologne, New Jersey post office from which her mail was always forwarded. The letters are touching: "My Dear Peace, I have just now heard of your death from this earthly body . . . If this is not so, please write back." Another wrote, "I know you are one with God . . . I see you in the Universe . . . "

An editor who had interviewed her in the 1960s and became a good friend wrote, " . . . cycles of prayer go on in my heart, telling her of my appreciation for her teaching and impact and influence on my life, wishing her well on her journey . . . "

A friend in Massachusetts wrote, "It was a great shock, to say the least, as well as a great loss for our little planet! My heart is full at this time for I, like thousands of other people, loved Peace so much! But at the same time I feel her presence will always be among us through her beautiful teachings and the life she exemplified . . . "

Many have written hoping that a book would be put together to help spread her special message of peace and love. A few others have said that they are thinking of writing articles or longer works about her. We hope this book will be a valuable resource for these and future writers, as well as an inspiration and encouragement to those who never had the good fortune to meet her.

One who captured her spirit wrote, "The seeds of peace have been scattered well. It is the duty of all who were touched by her to begin the harvest."

It is our hope that her words and spirit will continue to inspire. And we join with you in a circle of love, with all others who knew her and were touched by her . . .

> *Free of earth, as free as air,*
> *Now you travel everywhere.*

—Five of Peace's many friends
Santa Fe, New Mexico
March 31, 1982

CHAPTER 1

Growing Up

I HAD A VERY FAVORABLE BEGINNING, although many of you might not think so. I was born poor on a small farm on the outskirts of a small town, and I'm thankful for that. I was happy in my childhood. I had a woods to play in and a creek to swim in and room to grow. I wish that every child could have growing space because I think children are a little like plants. If they grow too close together they become thin and sickly and never obtain maximum growth. We need room to grow.

We begin to prepare for the work that we have to do and customarily we have no idea what we are preparing for. So as a child I had no idea what I was preparing for. And yet, of course, I was in many respects preparing. I was preparing for the pilgrimage when I chose my rule of 'first things first' and began to set priorities in my life. It led to a very orderly life and it taught me self discipline — a very valuable lesson, without which I could never have walked a pilgrimage. I carried it right into my adult life.

I received no formal religious training as a child. (It would be less that I would have to undo from my mind later on!) My first view inside a church was when I was twelve years old and I looked through the doorway of a Catholic church to watch janitors clean the cathedral. When I was sixteen I entered a church for the first time to attend a wedding.

When I was a senior in high school I began to make my search for God, but all my efforts were in an outward direction. I went about inquiring, "What is God? What is God?" I was most inquisitive and I asked many questions of many people, but I never received any answers! However, I was not about to give up. Intellectually I could not find God on the outside, so I tried another approach. I took a long walk with my dog and pondered deeply upon the question. Then I went to bed and slept over it. And in the morning I had my answer from the inside, through a still small voice.

Now my high school answer was a very simple answer — that we human beings just lump together everything in the universe which is beyond the capacity of all of us, and to all those things together some of us give the name God. Well, that set me on a search. And the first thing I did was to look at a tree, and I said, *there's one*. All of us working together couldn't create that one tree, and even if it looked like a tree it wouldn't grow. There is a creative force beyond us. And then I looked at my beloved stars at night and *there's another*. There's a sustaining power that keeps planets in their orbit.

I watched all the changes taking place in the universe. At that time they were trying to keep a lighthouse from washing into the sea. They finally moved it inland and said they had saved it. But I noticed all these changes and I said, *there's another*. There is something motivating towards constant change in the universe.

When I reached confirmation from within I knew beyond all doubt that I had touched my highest light.

Intellectually I touched God many times as truth and emotionally I touched God as love. I touched God as goodness. I touched God as kindness. It came to me that God is a creative force, a motivating power, an over-all intelligence, an ever-present, all pervading spirit — which binds everything in the universe together and gives life to everything. That brought God close. I could not be where God is not. *You are within God. God is within you.*

∅

I was working in the five-and-ten-cent store between my junior and senior year in high school. I just loved the work, especially fixing up counters so they would look pretty. They even let me fix up the windows because I liked to do that. Well, you know, I was cheaper than a window decorator!

I had two registers at my counter. One day I didn't have the proper change in one register so naturally I went over to the other and rang "no sale" and took out the change. Then I discovered I had committed a cardinal sin. I heard them whispering, "She rang 'no sale'!" The male floorwalker came over and said, "Come with me." He put me at a counter in a corner that needed fixing up. He left me there, and then came back and said, "Why did you do that?" I replied, "I still don't know what I did. I just took change out of the register — I didn't steal any money." He said, "You were instructed never to ring 'no sale'." I answered, "I wasn't instructed at all."

Then he went to the female floorwalker who was supposed to instruct me. I was reinstated. But, because of the incident, she then hated me. I knew that something needed to be done about it. Then I passed her desk and noticed a few faded flowers there. The next morning I brought her a beautiful bouquet of flowers from my garden. I said, "I noticed those faded flowers. I know you love flowers and here are some from my garden." She couldn't resist them. At the end of the week we walked out of there arm in arm!

I feel sure I was being prepared for the pilgrimage when I read the Golden Rule in history, "Do unto others what you would have others do unto you" — expressed in a lot of different ways and pointing out that every culture had one. It got an inner confirmation from me. It affected my entire life. In fact, there were certain offshoots of the Golden Rule which carried over even into the pilgrimage. When I was in high school I had a little saying, *If you want to make friends, you must be friendly.* If you analyze it, that is an offshoot of the Golden Rule. It is a recognition that people react according to the influences brought to bear upon them. I have it in my life today with my little saying, *If you want to make peace, you must be peaceful.*

I put the Golden Rule into practice just beyond my student days. I was given a job that one of my girl friends wanted, and I was elected to an office in the community club that she also wanted. She thought she hated me. She said all kinds of mean things about me. I knew it was a very unhealthy situation. So I hauled out the Golden Rule — I thought of and said every possible kind thing that could truthfully be said about her. I tried to do her favors. It fell to my lot to do her a significant favor. And to make a long story short, when she was married a year later I was maid of honor at her wedding. See how a little bit of spiritual practice goes a long way?

I know I was being prepared for the pilgrimage when I made certain choices. For instance, I was in grammar school when I was offered cigarettes from a package, which I did not smoke but my friends did. In high school I was offered all kinds of alcohol, which I did not drink but my friends did. Then just after my student days I was faced with a kind of test because all of my friends at that time used both alcohol and tobacco. There was such a push toward conformity in those days — they call it peer pressure now — that they actually looked down on me because I didn't do these things. And gathered in someone's living room I said to them, "Look, life is a series of choices and nobody can stop you from making your choices, but I have a right to make my own choices, too. And I have chosen freedom."

ℐ

I also made two very important discoveries as time went on. In the first place, I discovered that making money was easy. I had been led to believe that money and possessions would insure me a life of happiness and peace of mind. So that was the path I pursued. In the second place, I discovered that making money and spending it foolishly was completely meaningless. I knew that this was not what I was here for, but at that time I didn't know exactly what I was here for.

It was really the realization that money and things would not make me happy that got me started on my preparation for the pilgrimage. You may wonder how in the world I got involved with money and things in the first place, but you see, we are taught these sets of opposites which are extremely confusing.

I was very fortunate in that I was only confused by one of these sets of opposites; most people are confused by both.

On the one hand I was trained to believe that I should be kind and loving and never hurt anybody, which is fine. On the other hand I was trained to believe that if so ordered it is indeed honorable to maim and kill people in war. They even give medals for it. Now that one did not confuse me. I never believed there was any time under any circumstances when it was right for me to hurt anybody. But the other set of opposites confused me for awhile.

I was trained to be generous and unselfish and at the same time trained to believe that if I wanted to be successful I must get out there and grab more than my share of this world's goods. These conflicting philosophies which I had gathered from my childhood environment confused me for some time. But eventually I uprooted this false training.

CHAPTER 2:

The Spiritual Growing Up: My Steps Towards Inner Peace

As I LOOKED ABOUT THE WORLD, so much of it impoverished, I became increasingly uncomfortable about having so much while my brothers and sisters were starving. Finally I had to find another way. The turning point came when, in desperation and out of a very deep seeking for a meaningful way of life, I walked all one night through the woods. I came to a moonlit glade and prayed.

I felt a complete willingness, without any reservations, to give my life — to dedicate my life — to service. "Please use me!" I prayed to God. And a great peace came over me.

I tell you it's a point of no return. After that, you can never go back to completely self-centered living.

And so I went into the second phase of my life. I began to live to *give* what I could, instead of to get what I could, and I entered a new and wonderful world. My life began to be meaningful. I attained the great blessing of good health; I haven't had an ache or pain, a cold or headache since. (Most illness, you know, is psychologically induced.) From that time on, I have known that my life work would be for peace — that it would cover the *whole peace picture:* peace among nations, peace among groups, peace among individuals, and the very, very important inner peace. However,

7

there's a great deal of difference between being *willing* to give your life and actually *giving* your life, and for me fifteen years of preparation and inner seeking lay between.

I was not far down the spiritual road when I became acquainted with what the psychologists refer to as ego and conscience, which I call the lower self and the higher self, or the self-centered nature and the God-centered nature. It's as though we have two selves or natures or two wills with two contrary viewpoints.

Your lower self sees things from the viewpoint of your physical well-being only — your higher self considers your psychological or spiritual well-being. Your lower self sees you as the center of the universe — your higher self sees you as a cell in the body of humanity. When you are governed by your lower self you are selfish and materialistic, but insofar as you follow the promptings of your higher self you will see things realistically and find harmony within yourself and others.

The body, mind and emotions are instruments which can be used by either the self-centered nature or the God-centered nature. The self-centered nature uses these instruments, yet it is never fully able to control them, so there is a constant struggle. They can only be fully controlled by the God-centered nature.

When the God-centered nature takes over, you have found inner peace. Until that time comes, a partial control can be gained through discipline. It can be discipline imposed from without through early training which has become a part of the subconscious side of the self-centered nature. It can be discipline undertaken voluntarily: self-discipline. Now, if you are doing things you know you shouldn't do and don't really want to do, you certainly lack discipline. I recommend spiritual growing — and in the meantime self-discipline.

During the spiritual growing up period the inner conflict can be more or less stormy. Mine was about average. The self-centered nature is a very formidable enemy and it struggles fiercely to retain its identity. It defends itself in a cunning manner and should not be regarded lightly. It knows the weakest spots of your armor and attempts a confrontation when one is least aware. During these periods of attack, maintain a humble stature and be intimate with none but the guiding whisper of your higher self.

The higher self has been given many wonderful names by religious leaders, some calling the higher governing power the *inner light*, or the *indwelling Christ*. When Jesus said, "The Kingdom of God is within you," he was obviously referring to the higher self. In another place it says, *Christ in you, your hope of glory, the indwelling Christ*. Jesus was called the Christ because his life was governed by this higher governing power.

𝄞

When I talk about my steps toward inner peace, I talk about them in a framework, but there's nothing arbitrary about the number of steps. They can be expanded; they can be contracted. This is just a way of talking about the subject, but this is important: the steps toward inner peace are not taken in any certain order. The first step for one may be the last step for another. So just take whatever steps seem easiest for you, and as you take a few steps, it will become easier for you to take a few more. In this area we can really share. None of you may feel guided to walk a pilgrimage, and I'm not trying to inspire you to do so. But in the field of finding harmony in our own lives, we can share. And I suspect that when you hear me give some of the steps toward inner peace, you will recognize them as steps that you also have taken.

Preparations.

I would like to mention some preparations that were required of me. The first preparation is to take *a right attitude toward life*. This means, stop being an escapist! Stop being a surface liver who stays right in the froth of the surface. There are millions of these people, and they never find anything really worthwhile. Be willing to face life squarely and get down beneath the surface of life where the verities and realities are to be found. That's what we are doing here now.

There's the whole matter of having a meaningful attitude toward the problems that life may set before you. If only you could see the whole picture, if you knew the whole story, you would realize that no problem ever comes to you that does not have a purpose in your life, that cannot contribute to your inner growth. When you perceive this, you will recognize that problems are opportunities in disguise. If you did not face problems, you would just drift through life. It is through solving problems in accordance with the highest light we have that inner growth is attained. Now, collective problems must be solved by us collectively, and no one finds inner peace who avoids doing his or her share in the solving of collective problems, like world disarmament and world peace. So let us always think about these problems together and talk about them together, and collectively work toward their solutions.

The second preparation has to do with *bringing our lives into harmony with the laws that govern this universe.* Created are not only the worlds and the beings, but also the laws that govern them. Applying both in the physical realm and in the psychological realm, these laws govern human conduct. Insofar as we are able to understand and bring our lives into harmony with these laws, our lives will be in harmony. Insofar as we disobey these laws, we create difficulties for ourselves by our disobedience. We are our own worst enemies. If we are out of harmony through ignorance, we suffer somewhat; but if we know better and are still out of harmony, then we suffer a great deal. Suffering pushes us toward obedience.

I recognized that there are some well-known, little understood, and seldom practiced laws that we must live by if we wish to find peace within or without. Included are the laws that evil can only be overcome by good; that only good means can attain a good end; that those who do unloving things hurt themselves spiritually.

These laws are the same for all human beings and must be obeyed before harmony can prevail.

So I got busy on a very interesting project. This was to live all the good things I believed in. I did not confuse myself by trying to take them all at once, but rather if I was doing something that I knew I shouldn't be doing I stopped doing it and I always made a quick relinquishment. That's the easy way. Tapering off is long and hard. And if I was not doing something that I knew I should be doing, I got busy on that. It took the living quite a while to catch up with the believing, but of course. it can, and now if I believe something, I live it. Otherwise it would be perfectly meaningless. As I lived according to the *highest light* I had, I discovered that *other light* was given; that I opened myself to receiving more light as I lived the light I had.

𝒥

There is a third preparation that has to do with something which is unique for every human life, because every one of us has *a special place in the Life Pattern,* and no two people have exactly the same part to play in God's plan. There is a guidance which comes from within to all who will listen. Through this guidance each one will feel drawn to some part in the scheme of things.

God's laws can be known from within, but they can also be learned from without, as they have been spoken of by all great religious teachers. God's *guidance* can only be known from within.

We must remain open to God's guidance. God never guides us to break divine law, and if such a negative guidance comes to us we can be sure it is not from God. It is up to us to keep our lives steadfastly in harmony with divine law, which is the same for all of us. Only insofar as we remain in harmony with divine law do good things come to us.

When you come into this world your jobs in the divine plan are there. They just need to be realized and lived. If you do not yet know where you fit, I suggest that you try seeking it in receptive silence. I used to walk amid the beauties of nature, just receptive and silent, and wonderful insights would come to me.

You begin to do your part in the Life Pattern by doing all of the good things you feel motivated toward, even though they are just little good things at first. You give these priority in your life over all the superficial things that customarily clutter human lives.

Every morning I thought of God and thought of things I might do that day to be of service to God's children. I looked at every situation I came into to see if there was anything I could do there to be of service. I did as many good things as I could each day, not forgetting the importance of a pleasant word and a cheery smile. I prayed about things that seemed too big for me to handle — and right prayer motivates to right action.

I was filled with a runaway enthusiasm to help others, and one could argue that when I solved so many problems for others I was depriving them of the spiritual growth problem-solving brings. I soon realized I had to leave some good works for others to do and be blessed by.

In the beginning I helped people in simple ways with errands, gardening projects, and by reading to them. I spent some time in the private homes of the elderly and the recuperating ill, assisting them to overcome their various ailments. I worked with troubled teenagers, the psychologically disturbed, and the physically and mentally handicapped. My motives were pure and much of my work did have a positive and good effect. I used what I call spiritual therapy: I found all the good things that those I worked with wanted to do, and I helped them to do those things. There were some who became too attached to me and I had to work on breaking the attachment.

My lack of expertise was more than offset by the love I extended to others. When love fills your life all limitations are gone. The medicine this sick world needs so badly is love.

I also did some volunteer work for the American Friends Service Committee, the Women's International League for Peace and Freedom, and the Fellowship of Reconciliation — over a period of at least ten years, off and on.

There are those who know and do not do. This is very sad. In this materialistic age we have such a false criterion by which to measure success. We measure it in terms of dollars, in terms of material things. But happiness and inner peace do not lie in that direction. If you *know* but do not *do,* you are a very unhappy person indeed.

✵

There is a fourth preparation. It is *the simplification of life,* to bring inner and outer well-being, psychological and material well-being, into harmony in your life. This was made very easy for me. Just after I dedicated my life to service, I felt that I could no longer accept *more* than I need while others in the world have *less* than they need. This moved me to bring my life down to *need level*. I thought it would be difficult. I thought it would entail a great many hardships, but I was quite wrong. Instead of hardships, I found a wonderful sense of peace and joy, and a conviction that unnecessary possessions are only unnecessary burdens.

During this period I was able to meet my expenses on ten dollars a week, dividing my budget into two categories. I allocated $6.50 for food and incidentals and $3.50 for lodging.

Now I do not mean that needs are all the same. Your needs may be much greater than mine. For instance, if you have a family, you would need the stability of a family center for your children. But I do mean that anything beyond need — and need sometimes includes things beyond physical needs, too — anything beyond need tends to become burdensome. If you have it, you have to take care of it!

There is great freedom in simplicity of living, and after I began to feel this, I found harmony in my life between inner and outer well-being. There is a great deal to be said about such harmony, not only for an individual life but also for the life of a society. It's because as a world we have gotten ourselves so far out of harmony, so way off on the material side, that when we discover something like nuclear energy we are still capable of putting it into a bomb and using it to kill people! This is because our inner well-being lags so far behind our outer well-being. The valid research for the future is on the *inner* side, on the spiritual side, so that we will be able to bring these two into balance — and so that we will know how to use well the outer well-being we already have.

Purifications.

Then I discovered that there were some purifications required of me. The first one is such a simple thing: it is *purification of the body*. This had to do with my physical living habits. I used to eat all the standard foods. I shudder now to think of what I used to dump into this temple of the spirit.

I did not take care of my bodily temple when I was very young; this only happened later in life. It was five years after I felt a complete willingness to give my life that I began to take care of my bodily temple — *five years!* Now I eat mostly fruits, nuts, vegetables, whole grains (preferably organically grown) and perhaps a bit of milk and cheese. This is what I live on and walk on.

There was a time when I had the caffeine habit. I would get up in the morning and have my cup of coffee first thing. One morning, when I had just taken my cup of coffee, I sat and looked at that coffee cup and said, "You're depending on *that* to get you perking in the morning! I'm not going to be a slave to caffeine. This is going to stop right here!" And it did. I never touched it again. I missed it for a few days, but I'm stronger than that cup of coffee!

I began to realize that I was disobeying my rule of life which says: *I will not ask anyone to do for me things that I would refuse to do for myself.* Now, I wouldn't kill any creature — I wouldn't even kill a chicken or a fish — and therefore I stopped immediately eating all flesh.

I have not eaten flesh for many years, not meat or fish or fowl. I have learned since that it is bad for your health, but at that time I just extended my love to include not only all my fellow human beings but also my fellow creatures, and so I stopped hurting them and I stopped eating them.

I did not know at that time that flesh eating was bad for the spirit. I just knew it was something I could no longer do because it was contrary to one of my rules of life. Then I learned a little later from a doctor that flesh eating leaves poisonous residues in the body, which would also have made me a vegetarian. I believe in practicing prevention since the body is the temple of the spirit.

Then I learned from a college professor, who wrote a book on the subject, that it takes many times the land to raise the creatures we eat as it would to raise fruits or vegetables or grains. Since I want the maximum number of God's children to be fed, that also would make me a vegetarian.

The difficulty is we have not learned to stop killing *each other* yet. That's our present lesson — not to kill each other. To learn the lesson of sharing and the lesson of non-killing of man by man. The lesson of non-killing of creatures is a little bit into the future, though those of us who know better need to live up to our highest light.

When I realized white flour and white sugar were bad for your health I stopped eating them. When I realized highly seasoned things were bad I quit them. And when I realized all processed foods contain substances that are bad for the body I quit eating them. Even most water out of the tap is a chemical cocktail. I would suggest bottled or distilled water.

I know enough about food to nourish my body properly and I have excellent health. I enjoy my food, but I eat to live. I do not live to eat, as some people do, and I know when to stop eating. I am not enslaved by food.

People can still be hungry after eating large quantities of wrong foods. In fact, you can suffer from malnutrition even though you consistently overeat wrong foods. You can begin a healthy diet by having only good, wholesome foods available. Eat slowly and chew your food well, as I do. Then make food a very incidental part of your life by filling your life so full of meaningful things that you'll hardly have time to think about food.

In my eating and sleeping habits I have the closest contact with nature that is possible for me. Each day I get as much fresh air and sunshine and contact with nature as I can. I want to do much of my living out-of-doors and be a part of the landscape. Rest and exercise are important. I am not one who consistently goes without sleep. When possible, I go to bed at dusk and get eight hours of sleep. I take my exercise by walking and swinging my arms which makes it a complete form of exercise.

You'd think purification of the body might be the first area in which people would be willing to work, but from practical experience I've discovered it's often the last — because it might mean getting rid of some of our bad habits, and there is nothing we cling to more tenaciously.

There is a second purification: *purification of thought.* If you realized how powerful your thoughts are, you would never think a negative thought. They can be a powerful influence for good when they're on the positive side, and they can and do make you physically ill when they're on the negative side. I don't eat junk foods and I don't think junk thoughts! Let me tell you, junk thoughts can destroy you even more quickly than junk food. Junk thoughts are something to be wary of.

Let me tell you a story of a man adversely affected by negative thoughts. He was sixty-five years old when I knew him and he was manifesting symptoms of what was called a chronic physical illness. When I talked to him I realized there was some bitterness in his life. However, I couldn't put my finger on it right away because I saw he was getting along well with his wife, his grown children and the folks in his community. But the bitterness was there just the same. I found that he was harboring bitterness against his father who had been dead for many long years because his father had educated his brother and not him. He was a very intellectual person so I talked to him at length. When he, the oldest son, was to be educated, his father had absolutely not enough money to do it. In fact, the family was very poor at that time. There were several sisters after him and I think three of them hadn't been educated either. His brother was the youngest, and by that time his father had more money and was able to educate the brother. He didn't begrudge his brother the education, he just thought he should have gotten it too. When he saw intellectually that his father had done the best he could with both of his sons, then he was able to release the bitterness he had been harboring. That so-called chronic illness began to fade away and soon the condition was much improved and then it was gone.

If you're harboring the slightest bitterness toward anyone, or any unkind thoughts of any sort whatever, you must get rid of them quickly. They are not hurting anyone but you. It isn't enough just to do right things and say right things — you must also *think* right things before your life can come into harmony.

ॐ

During the preparation period I wasn't fully identifying with the real me, I was just learning. I was very forgiving toward others, that was no problem, but I was very unforgiving toward myself. If I did something that wasn't the highest, I would say to myself, "You ought to know better." And then one day as I was combing my hair at the mirror, I looked at myself and said, "You vain thing! Why do you think you know better when you forgive everyone else for not knowing better? You're not any better than they are."

You must learn to forgive yourself as easily as you forgive others. And then take a further step and use all that energy that you used in condemning yourself for improving yourself. After that I really started to get somewhere — because there's only one person you can change and that's yourself. After you have changed yourself, you might be able to inspire others to look for change.

It took the living quite awhile to catch up with the believing, but it finally did. And when it did, a progress began which never ended. As I lived up to the highest light I had, higher and higher light came to me.

ॐ

The third purification is *the purification of desire*. What are the things you desire? Do you desire superficial things like pleasures — new items of wearing apparel or new household furnishings or cars? Since you are here to get yourself in harmony with the laws that govern human conduct and with your part in the scheme of things, your desires should be focused in this direction. It's very important to get your desires *centered* so you will desire only to do God's will for you. You can come to the point of oneness of desire, just to know and do your part in the Life Pattern. When you think about it, is there anything else as really important to desire?

There is one more purification, and that is *purification of motive*. What is your motive for whatever you may be doing? If it is pure greed or self-seeking or the wish for self-glorification, I would say, *don't do that thing*. Don't do anything you would do with such a motive. But that isn't easy because we tend to do things with very mixed motives. I've never found a person who had purely bad motives. There may be such a person, I have never encountered one. I do encounter people who constantly have mixed motives. Good and bad motives all mixed together. For instance, I met a man in the business world and he admitted that his motives were not the highest, and yet mixed in with them were good motives — providing for his family, doing some good in his community. Mixed motives!

I talk to groups studying the most advanced spiritual teachings and sometimes these people wonder why nothing is happening in their lives. Their motive is the attainment of inner peace for themselves — which of course is a selfish motive. You will not find it with this motive. The motive, if you are to find inner peace, must be an outgoing motive. Service, of course, *service*. Giving, not getting. Your motive must be good if your work is to have good effect. The secret of life is being of service.

I knew a man who was a good architect. It was obviously his right work, but he was doing it with the wrong motive. His motive was to make a lot of money and to keep ahead of the Joneses. He worked himself into an illness, and it was shortly after that I met him. I got him to do little things for service. I talked to him about the joy of service and I knew that after he had experienced this he could never go back into really self-centered living. We corresponded a bit after that. A few years later I hardly recognized him when I stopped in to see him. He was such a changed man! But he was still an architect. He was drawing a plan and he talked to me about it: "You see, I'm designing it this way to fit into their budget, and then I'll set it on their plot of ground to make it look nice . . . " His motive was to be of service to the people he drew plans for. He was a radiant and transformed person. His wife told me that his business had increased because people were now coming to him from miles around for home designs.

I've met a few people who had to change their jobs in order to change their lives, but I've met many more people who merely had to change their motive to service in order to change their lives.

Relinquishments.

Now, the last part deals with relinquishments. Once you've made the first relinquishment you have found inner peace, because it's *the relinquishment of self-will.*

You can work on subordinating the lower self by refraining from doing the not-good things you may be motivated toward — not suppressing them, but transforming them so that the higher self can take over your life. If you are motivated to do or say a mean thing, you can always think of a good thing. You deliberately turn around and use that *same energy* to do or say a good thing instead. It works!

𝒥

The second relinquishment is *the relinquishment of the feeling of separateness.* We begin feeling very separate and judging everything as it relates to us, as though we were the center of the universe. Even after we know better intellectually, we still judge things that way. In reality, of course, we are all cells in the body of humanity. We are not separate from our fellow humans. The whole thing is a totality. It's only from that higher viewpoint that you can know what it is to love your neighbor as yourself. From that higher viewpoint there becomes just one realistic way to work, and that is for the good of the whole. As long as you work for your selfish little self, you're just one cell against all those other cells, and you're way out of harmony. But as soon as you begin working for the good of the whole, you find yourself in harmony with all of your fellow human beings. You see, it's the easy, harmonious way to live.

🍏

Then there is the third relinquishment, and that is *the relinquishment of all attachments.* No one is truly free who is still attached to material things, or to places, or to people. Material things must be put into their proper place. They are there for use. It's all right to use them, that's what they're there for. But when they've outlived their usefulness, be ready to relinquish them and perhaps pass them on to someone who does need them. Anything that you cannot relinquish when it has outlived its usefulness possesses you, and in this materialistic age a great many of us are possessed by our possessions. We are not free.

I considered myself liberated long before it became the fashion. First I liberated myself from debilitating habits, and went on to free myself of combative, aggressive thoughts. I have also cast aside any unnecessary possessions. This, I feel, is true liberation.

There is another kind of possessiveness. *You do not possess any other human being,* no matter how closely related that other may be. No husband owns his wife; no wife owns her husband; no parents own their children. When we think we possess people there is a tendency to run their lives for them, and out of this develop extremely inharmonious situations. Only when we realize that we do not possess them, that they must live in accordance with their own inner motivations, do we stop trying to run their lives for them, and then we discover that we are able to live in harmony with them. Anything that you strive to hold captive will hold you captive — and if you desire freedom you must give freedom.

Associations formed in this earth life are not necessarily for the duration of the life span. Separation takes place constantly, and as long as it takes place *lovingly* not only is there no spiritual injury, but spiritual progress may actually be helped.

We must be able to appreciate and enjoy the places where we tarry and yet pass on without anguish when we are called elsewhere. In our spiritual development we are often required to pull up roots many times and to close many chapters in our lives until we are no longer attached to any material thing and can love all people without any attachment to them.

♫

Now the last: *the relinquishment of all negative feelings*. I want to mention just one negative feeling which the nicest people still experience, and that negative feeling is *worry*. Worry is not *concern*, which would motivate you to do everything possible in a situation. Worry is a useless mulling over of things we cannot change.

One final comment about negative feelings, which helped me very much at one time and has helped others. No outward thing — nothing, nobody from without — can hurt me inside, psychologically. I recognized that I could only be hurt psychologically by my own wrong actions, which I have control over; by my own wrong *reactions* (they are tricky, but I have control over them too); or by my own *inaction* in some situations, like the present world situation, that need action from me. When I recognized all this how free I felt! And I just stopped hurting myself. Now someone could do the meanest thing to me and I would feel deep compassion for this out-of-harmony person, this sick person, who is capable of doing mean things. I certainly would not hurt myself by a wrong reaction of bitterness or anger. You have complete control over whether you will be psychologically hurt or not, and anytime you want to, you can stop hurting yourself.

♫

These are my steps toward inner peace that I wanted to share with you. There is nothing new about this. This is universal truth. I merely talked about these things in everyday words in terms of my own personal experience with them. The laws which govern this universe work for good as soon as we obey them, and anything contrary to these laws doesn't last long. It contains within itself the seeds of its own destruction. The good in every human life always makes it possible for us to obey these laws. We do have free will about all this, and therefore how soon we obey and thereby find harmony, both within ourselves and within our world, is up to us.

♫

During this spiritual growing up period I desired to know and do God's will for me. Spiritual growth is not easily attained, but it is well worth the effort. It takes time, just as any growth takes time. One should rejoice at small gains and not be impatient, as impatience hampers growth.

The path of gradual relinquishment of things hindering spiritual progress is a difficult path, for only when relinquishment is complete do the rewards really come. The path of quick relinquishment is an easy path, for it brings immediate blessings. And when God fills your life, God's gifts overflow to bless all you touch.

To me, it was an escape from the artificiality of illusion into the richness of reality. To the world it may seem that I had given up much. I had given up burdensome possessions, spending time meaninglessly, doing things I knew I should not do and not doing things I knew I should do. But to me it seemed that I had gained much — even the priceless treasures of health and happiness.

The Attainment of Inner Peace.

There were hills and valleys, lots of hills and valleys, in that spiritual growing up period. Then in the midst of the struggle there came a wonderful mountaintop experience — the first glimpse of what the life of inner peace was like.

That came when I was out walking in the early morning. All of a sudden I felt very uplifted, more uplifted than I had ever been. I remember I knew *timelessness* and *spacelessness* and *lightness*. I did not seem to be walking on the earth. There were no people or even animals around, but every flower, every bush, every tree seemed to wear a halo. There was a light emanation around everything and flecks of gold fell like slanted rain through the air. This experience is sometimes called the illumination period.

The most important part of it was not the phenomena: the important part of it was the realization of the oneness of all creation. Not only all human beings — I knew before that all human beings are one. But now I knew also a oneness with the rest of creation. The creatures that walk the earth and the growing things of the earth. The air, the water, the earth itself. And, most wonderful of all, *a oneness with that which permeates all and binds all together and gives life to all.* A oneness with that which many would call God.

I have never felt separate since. I could return again and again to this wonderful mountaintop, and then I could stay there for longer and longer periods of time and just slip out occasionally.

𝔍

The inspiration for the pilgrimage came at this time. I sat high upon a hill overlooking rural New England. The day before I had slipped out of harmony, and the evening before I had thought to God, "It seems to me that if I could always remain in harmony I could be of greater usefulness — for every time I slip out of harmony it impairs my usefulness."

When I awoke at dawn I was back on the spiritual mountaintop with a wonderful feeling. I knew that I would never need to descend again into the valley. I knew that for me the struggle was over, that finally I had succeeded in giving my life or finding inner peace. Again this is a point of no return. You can never go back into the struggle. The struggle is over now because you *will* to do the right thing and you don't need to be pushed into it.

I went out for a time alone with God. While I was out a thought struck my mind: I felt a strong inner motivation toward the pilgrimage — toward this special way of witnessing for peace.

I saw, in my mind's eye, myself walking along and wearing the garb of my mission . . . I saw a map of the United States with the large cities marked — and it was as though someone had taken a colored crayon and marked a zigzag line across, coast to coast and border to border, from Los Angeles to New York City. I knew what I was to do. And that was a vision of my first year's pilgrimage route in 1953!

I entered a new and wonderful world. My life was blessed with a meaningful purpose.

𝔍

However, progress was not over. Great progress has taken place in this third phase of my life. It's as though the central figure of the jigsaw puzzle of my life is complete and clear and unchanging, and around the edges other pieces keep fitting in. There is always a growing edge, but the progress is harmonious. There is a feeling of always being surrounded by all of the good things, like love and peace and joy. It seems like a protective surrounding, and there is an unshakeableness within which takes you through any situation you may need to face.

The world may look at you and believe that you are facing great problems, but always there are the inner resources to easily overcome the problems. Nothing seems difficult. There is a calmness and a serenity and unhurriedness — no more striving or straining about anything. That's a very important thing I've learned. If your life is in harmony with your part in the Life Pattern, and if you are obedient to the laws which govern this universe, then life is full and life is good but life is nevermore overcrowded. If it is overcrowded, then you are doing more than is right for you to do — more than is your job to do in the total scheme of things.

Now there is a living to give instead of to get. As you concentrate on the giving, you discover that just as you cannot receive without giving, so neither can you give without receiving — even the most wonderful things like health and happiness and inner peace. There is a feeling of endless energy, it just never runs out, it seems to be as endless as air. You seem to be *plugged in* to the source of universal energy.

You are now in control of your life. Your higher nature, which is controlled by God, controls the body, mind, and emotions. (The ego is never really in control. The ego is controlled by wishes for comfort and convenience on the part of the body, by demands of the mind, and by outbursts of the emotions.)

I can say to my body, "Lie down there on that cement floor and go to sleep," and it obeys. I can say to my mind, "Shut out everything else and concentrate on the job before you," and it is obedient. I can say to my emotions, "Be still, even in the face of this terrible situation," and they are still. A great philosopher has said, *he who seems to be out of step may be following a different drummer.* And now you are following a different drummer: the higher nature instead of the lower nature.

When you have done the spiritual growing up you realize that every human being is of equal importance, has work to do in this world, and has equal potential. We are in many varied stages of growth; this is true because we have free will. You have free will as to whether you will finish the mental and emotional growing up. Many choose not to. You have free will as to whether you will begin the spiritual growing up. The beginning of it is the time when you feel completely willing, without any reservations, to leave the self-centered life. And most choose not to. But it was doing that growth and finding inner peace that prepared me for the pilgrimage that I walk today.

ॐ

Looking through the eyes of the divine nature you see the essence within the manifestation, the creator within the creation, and it is a wonderful, wonderful world!

ॐ

I realized in 1952 that it was the proper time for a pilgrim to step forth. The war in Korea was raging and the McCarthy era was at its height. It was a time when congressional committees considered people guilty until they could prove their innocence. There was great fear at that time and it was safest to be apathetic. Yes, it was most certainly a time for a pilgrim to step forward, because a pilgrim's job is to rouse people from apathy and make them think.

With the last bit of money I had left, I bought not only paper and stencil for my first messages but material for my first tunic. Although I designed it, the sewing was done by a lady in California, and the lettering was painted by a man who was a sign painter. My initial reaction when I first put it on was a wonderful 'rightness' about it, and I immediately accepted it.

CHAPTER 3:

The Pilgrimage

A PILGRIM IS A WANDERER WITH A PURPOSE. A pilgrimage can be to a place — that's the best known kind — but it can also be for a thing. Mine is for peace, and that is why I am a Peace Pilgrim.

My pilgrimage covers the entire peace picture: peace among nations, peace among groups, peace within our environment, peace among individuals, and the very, very important inner peace — which I talk about most often because that is where peace begins.

The situation in the world around us is just a reflection of the collective situation. In the final analysis, only as we become more peaceful people will we be finding ourselves living in a more peaceful world.

In the middle ages the pilgrims went out as the disciples were sent out — without money, without food, without adequate clothing — and I know that tradition. I have no money. I do not accept any money on my pilgrimage. I belong to no organization. There is no organization backing me. I own only what I wear and carry. There is nothing to tie me down. I am as free as a bird soaring in the sky.

I walk until given shelter, fast until given food. I don't ask — it's given without asking. Aren't people good! There is a spark of good in everybody, no matter how deeply it may be buried, it is there. It's waiting to govern your life gloriously. I call it the God-centered nature or the divine nature. Jesus called it the Kingdom of God within.

Now, a pilgrim walks prayerfully, and a pilgrim walks as an opportunity to come in contact with many people and perhaps inspire them to do something for peace in their own way. For that purpose I wear my short tunic with *PEACE PILGRIM* on the front and *25,000 Miles On Foot for Peace* on the back. It makes my contacts for me in the kindest way . . . and I like to be kind.

You're in a much better position to talk with people when they approach you than when you approach them. Those individuals who are attracted to me are either genuinely interested in some phase of peace or just have a good lively curiosity. Both kinds are very worthwhile people. Then I have time to share with people my peace message which says in one sentence:

> *This is the way of peace — overcome evil with good,*
> *and falsehood with truth, and hatred with love.*

The Golden Rule would do equally well. There is nothing new about that except the practice of it. But I consider it the lesson for today and so it becomes the message of the peace pilgrimage. Please don't say lightly that these are just religious concepts and not practical. These are laws governing human conduct, which apply as rigidly as the law of gravity. When we disregard these laws in any walk of life, chaos results. Through obedience to these laws this world of ours will enter a period of peace and richness of life beyond our fondest dreams.

The key word for our time is *practice*. We have all the light we need, we just need to put it into practice.

ℐ

What I walk on is not the energy of youth, it is a better energy. I walk on the endless energy of inner peace that never runs out! When you become a channel through which God works there are no more limitations, because God does the work *through you*: you are merely the instrument — and what God can do is unlimited. When you are working for God you do not find yourself striving and straining. You find yourself calm, serene and unhurried.

My pilgrimage is not a crusade, which connotes violence. There is no attempt to force something on people. A pilgrimage is a gentle journey of prayer and example. My walking is first of all a prayer for peace. If you give your life as a prayer you intensify the prayer beyond all measure.

In undertaking this pilgrimage I do not think of myself as an individual but rather as an embodiment of the heart of the world which is pleading for peace. Humanity, with fearful, faltering steps walks a knife-edge between abysmal chaos and a new renaissance, while strong forces push toward chaos. Yet there is hope. I see hope in the tireless work of a few devoted souls. I see hope in the real desire for peace in the heart of humanity, even though the human family gropes toward peace blindly, not knowing the way.

My pilgrimage is an opportunity to talk with my fellow human beings about the way of peace. It is also a penance for whatever I may have contributed by commission or omission to the tragic situation in the world today. It is a prayer that this war-weary world of ours will somehow find the way to peace before a holocaust descends.

My mission is to help promote peace by helping others to find *inner peace*. If I can find it, you can too. Peace is an idea whose time has come.

♫

I began my pilgrimage on the first of January in 1953. It is my spiritual birthday of sorts. It was a period in which I was merged with the whole. No longer was I a seed buried under the ground, but I felt as a flower reaching out effortlessly toward the sun. On that day I became a wanderer relying upon the goodness of others. It would be a pilgrim's journey undertaken in the traditional manner: on foot and on faith. I left behind all claims to a name, personal history, possessions and affiliations.

It would be a glorious journey.

The birthplace of the pilgrimage was at the Tournament of Roses parade in Pasadena, California. I walked ahead along the line of march, talking to people and handing out peace messages, and noticing that the holiday spirit did not lessen the genuine interest in peace. When I had gone about half way a policeman put his hand on my shoulder and I thought he was going to tell me to get off the line of march. Instead he said, "What we need is thousands like you."

What happened to me in the Los Angeles area in the beginning was almost miraculous. All channels of communication were opened to me and my little peace message. I spent hours being interviewed by newspaper reporters and being photographed by newspaper photographers. The story of the pilgrimage and even my picture went out over all the wire services. Besides doing two live television programs, I spent hours recording for radio and the television newscasts.

Newspapers all along the line from Los Angeles to San Diego were interested. In San Diego I did one television program and four radio shows. The head of the San Diego Council of Churches approved of my message and my three petitions, and they were widely circulated in the churches.

꒰꒱

When I was not on the road I was speaking and gathering signatures for the three peace petitions which I carried. The first was a short plea for immediate peace in Korea. It read: *"Let the killing in Korea cease! Then deal with this conflict situation according to the only principles which can solve it — overcome evil with good and falsehood with truth and hatred with love."*

The second petition was directed to the President and congressional leaders requesting the installation of a Peace Department. It read: *"This is the way of peace, overcome evil with good and falsehood with truth and hatred with love. We plead for the establishment of a Peace Department, with a Secretary of Peace who accepts these principles — and with all conflicts at home and abroad to be referred to this Peace Department."*

The third petition was a plea to the United Nations and the world leaders for world disarmament and reconstruction: *"If you would find the way of peace you must overcome evil with good and falsehood with truth and hatred with love. We plead with you to free us all from the crushing burden of armaments, to free us from hatred and fear, so that we may feed our hungry ones, mend our broken cities, and experience a richness of life which can only come in a world that is unarmed and fed."*

I accumulated signed petitions from individuals, peace groups, churches and organizations along my pilgrimage route, storing them in a satchel which was carried for the occasion. I presented them to officials at both the White House and the United Nations at the conclusion of my first walk across the country. And I am thankful that my first petition, *"Let the killing in Korea cease ..."* was at least partially granted before the first year was over.

∬

At Tijuana, Mexico, just across the border from San Diego, I was received by the mayor, and he gave me a message to carry to the mayor of New York City. I also carried a message from the California Indians to the Arizona Indians.

While passing through San Diego that first year I was introduced into public speaking. A high school teacher approached me on the street and inquired if I would speak to her class. I told her in all fairness that as Peace Pilgrim I had never spoken to a group before. She assured me that it would be fine and asked only that I would answer the students' questions. I agreed. If you have something worthwhile to say, you can say it. Otherwise, why in the world would you want to be speaking?

I have no problem speaking before a group. When you have completely surrendered to God's will, the way seems easy and joyous. It is only before you have completely surrendered that the way seems difficult. When I speak, energy flows through me like electricity flows through a wire.

In the beginning, my speaking engagements were often arranged on the spur of the moment. As I was walking past a school, the principal came out and said, "My students are looking at you from the windows. If you would come in and talk to them we'll gather them in the gymnasium." So I did.

Then at noon, a man from one of the civic clubs approached me and said, "My speaker disappointed us. Will you come and speak at our luncheon?" And of course I did.

The same afternoon a college professor on the way to his class stopped me and asked, "Could I take you to my students?" So I spoke to his class.

Then at night a minister and his wife going to a church supper stopped me and said, "Would you consider coming and eating with us, and speaking to us?" And I did. They also gave me a bed for the night. And all this happened as I was walking along one day without any prior engagements.

I now keep very busy speaking for peace at colleges, high

schools, churches, and so forth — but always I am happily busy. My slogan of *First things first* has enabled me to take care of my speaking engagements, keep my mail up to date and also do some walking.

Once in Cincinnati I gave seven sermons at seven different places of worship in one day. On that particular Sunday I gave local ministers the day off!

No collections are permitted at meetings that are held for me. I never accept a penny for the work I do. Any money sent to me through the mail is used to publish my literature which is sent free of charge to anyone who requests it.

Truth is the pearl without price. One cannot obtain truth by buying it — all you can do is to strive for spiritual truth and when one is ready, it will be given freely. Nor should spiritual truth be sold, lest the seller be injured spiritually. You lose any spiritual contact the moment you commercialize it. Those who have the truth would not be packaging it and selling it, so anyone who is selling it, really does not possess it.

⌀

When I first started out I thought the pilgrimage might entail some hardships. But I was determined to live at need level, that is, *I didn't want more than I need when so many have less than they need.* Penance is the willingness to undergo hardships for the achievement of a good purpose. I was willing. But when hardships came I found myself lifted above them. Instead of hardship, I found a wonderful sense of peace and joy and conviction that I was following God's will. Blessings instead of hardships are showered upon me.

I remember my first lesson on the pilgrimage was the lesson of receiving. I had been on the giving side for many years and I needed to learn to accept as gracefully as I had been able to give, in order to give the other fellow the joy and blessing of giving. It's so beautiful when you live to give. To me it's the only way to live, because as you give you receive spiritual blessings.

I was tested severely in the beginning of my pilgrimage. Life is a series of tests; but if you pass your tests, you look back upon them as good experiences. I'm glad I had these experiences.

If you have a loving and positive attitude toward your fellow human beings, you will not fear them. *'Perfect love casteth out all fear.'*

One test happened in the middle of the night in the middle of the California desert. The traffic had just about stopped, and there wasn't a human habitation within many miles. I saw a car parked at the side of the road. The driver called to me saying, "Come on, get in and get warm." I said, "I don't ride." He said, "I'm not going anywhere, I'm just parked here." I got in. I looked at the man. He was a big, burly man — what most people would call a rough looking individual. After we had talked a while he said, "Say, wouldn't you like to get a few winks of sleep?" And I said, "Oh, yes, I certainly would!" And I curled up and went to sleep. When I awoke I could see the man was very puzzled about something, and after we had talked for quite some time he admitted that when he had asked me to get into the car he had certainly meant me no good, adding, "When you curled up so trustingly and went to sleep, I just couldn't touch you!"

I thanked him for the shelter and began walking away. As I looked back I saw him gazing at the heavens, and I hoped he had found God that night.

No one walks so safely as one who walks humbly and harmlessly with great love and great faith. For such a person gets through to the good in others (and there is good in everyone), and therefore cannot be harmed. This works between individuals, it works between groups and it would work between nations if nations had the courage to try it.

Once I was hit by a disturbed teenage boy whom I had taken for a walk. He wanted to go hiking but was afraid he might break a leg and be left lying there. Everyone was afraid to go with him. He was a great big fellow and looked like a football player, and he was known to be violent at times. He had once beaten his mother so badly that she had to spend several weeks in the hospital. Everybody was afraid of him, so I offered to go with him.

As we got up to the first hilltop everything was going fine. Then a thunderstorm came along. He was very terrified because the thundershower was very close. Suddenly he went off the beam and came for me, hitting at me. I didn't run away although I guess I could have — he had a heavy pack on his back. But even while he was hitting me I could only feel the deepest compassion toward him. How terrible to be so psychologically sick that you would be able to hit a defenseless old woman! I bathed his hatred with love even while he hit me. As a result the hitting stopped.

He said, "You didn't hit back! Mother always hits back." The delayed reaction, because of his disturbance, had reached the good in him. Oh, it's there — no matter how deeply it is buried — and he experienced remorse and complete self-condemnation.

What are a few bruises on my body in comparison with the transformation of a human life? To make a long story short he was never violent again. He is a useful person in this world today.

ℐ

On another occasion I was called upon to defend a frail eight year old girl against a large man who was about to beat her. The girl was terrified. It was my most difficult test. I was staying at a ranch and the family went into town. The little girl did not want to go with them, and they asked, since I was there, would I take care of the child? I was writing a letter by the window when I saw a car arrive. A man got out of the car. The girl saw him and ran and he followed, chasing her into a barn. I went immediately into the barn. The girl was cowering in terror in the corner. He was coming at her slowly and deliberately.

You know the power of thought. You're constantly creating through thought. And you attract to you whatever you fear. So I knew her danger because of her fear. (I fear nothing and expect good — so good comes!)

I put my body immediately between the man and the girl. I just stood and looked at this poor, psychologically sick man with loving compassion. He came close. He stopped! He looked at me for quite a while. He then turned and walked away and the girl was safe. There was not a word spoken.

Now, what was the alternative? Suppose I had been so foolish as to forget the law of love by hitting back and relying upon the jungle law of tooth and claw? Undoubtedly I would have been beaten — perhaps even to death and possibly the little girl as well! Never underestimate the power of God's love — it transforms! It reaches the spark of good in the other person and the person is disarmed.

ℐ

When I started out on my pilgrimage, I was using walking for two purposes at that time. One was to contact people, and I still use it for that purpose today. But the other was as a prayer discipline. To keep me concentrated on my prayer for peace. And after a few years I discovered something. I discovered that I no longer needed the prayer discipline. I pray without ceasing now. My personal prayer is: *Make me an instrument through which only truth can speak.*

∬

During my pilgrimage through Arizona I was arrested by a plainclothes policeman while mailing letters at the local post office in Benson. After a short ride in a patrol car I was booked as a vagrant. When you walk on faith you are technically guilty of vagrancy. Yes, I've been jailed several times for not having any money, but they always release me once they understand.

There is a great deal of difference between a prison and a jail. A prison is something big that maintains some kind of standards. A jail is a little affair that doesn't maintain much of any standard. And this was a jail!

They put me into a huge inner room surrounded by cell blocks in which they locked the women, four to a cell for the night. As I walked in I said to myself, "Peace Pilgrim, you have dedicated your life to service — behold your wonderful new field of service!"

When I walked in one of the girls said, "Gee, you're a funny one, you're the only one that came in smiling. Most of them come in crying or cursing."

I said to them, "Suppose you had a day off at home — wouldn't you do something worthwhile on that day?" They said, "Yes, what will we do?" So I got them to sing songs that lifted the spirit. I gave them a simple exercise which makes you feel tingly all over. Then I talked to them about the steps toward inner peace. I told them they lived in a community and what could be done in an outer community could also be done in their community. They were interested and asked many questions. Oh, it was a beautiful day.

At the end of the day they changed matrons. The girls didn't like the woman who came in. They said she was a horrible person and said not to even speak to her. But I know there's good in everybody and of course I spoke to her. I learned this woman was supporting her children with this job. She felt she had to work and didn't always feel well and that's why she was a bit cross at times. There is a reason for everything.

I asked the matron to visualize only the good in the inmates. And I asked the girls to visualize only the good in the beleaguered matron.

Later on I said to the matron, "I realize you have a full house here and I can sleep comfortably on this wooden bench." Instead she had them bring me a cot with clean bedclothes, and I had a warm shower with a clean towel and all the comforts of home.

In the morning I bade farewell to my friends and was escorted by a local deputy to the courthouse several blocks away. I wasn't handcuffed nor was he even holding onto me. But he had a great big gun at his side, and so I looked at him and said, "If I were to run away, would you shoot me?" "Oh, no," he said grinning, "I never shoot anything I can catch!"

In court that morning I pleaded not guilty and my case was immediately dismissed. In my personal effects which were taken overnight was a letter which had great weight in my release. It read: *"The bearer of this note has identified herself as a Peace Pilgrim walking coast to coast to direct the attention of our citizens to her desire for peace in the world. We do not know her personally as she is just passing through our state, but since undoubtedly it will be a long, hard trip for her, we wish her safe passage."* It was on official stationery and signed by the governor of the state, Howard Pyle.

When I was being released a court officer remarked, "You don't seem to be any the worse for your day in jail." I said, "You can imprison my body, but not the spirit." It's only the body they can put behind prison bars. I never felt in prison and neither will *you* ever feel in prison — unless you imprison yourself.

They took me to the spot where I had been picked up the day before. It was a beautiful experience.

Every experience is what you make it and it serves a purpose. It might inspire you, it might educate you, or it might come to give you a chance to be of service in some way.

⌀

Most of my speaking is now scheduled well in advance but I am still offered speaking engagements in a most unexpected manner. In Minneapolis I was being interviewed by a reporter at a gathering of civic club members who were awaiting an address by the Minnesota governor. He was unable to make it so they invited me to speak in his place. Of course I accepted!

And speaking of governors, as I stepped inside the big front door of a State House one day, a nice friendly gentleman greeted me and shook my hand and asked if he could help me. I told him I was looking for the Governor's office and he promptly took me there. "Is there anything else I can do to help you?" he asked. "I thought I might have the privilege of shaking hands with the Governor," I said. "You *have* shaken hands with the Governor," said the nice friendly gentleman — the Governor himself.

⁊

It was the first year of my pilgrimage and I was somewhere along the highway between El Paso and Dallas when I was picked up for vagrancy. I have never heard of the FBI investigating people for vagrancy but I was. A man in a black car stopped and showed me his badge. He didn't even demand that I come with him, he just said, "Will you come with me?"

I said, "Oh yes. I'll be interested in talking with you."

I got into his car, but first I scratched a large 'X' on the highway where I had been picked up. During the time I was counting miles, if I left the highway I would make a large 'X' and then return to the spot to begin my walk anew.

He took me to this prison and said, "Book her for vagrancy," and I went through the routine. They first take you in for finger-printing. I was fascinated because I never had fingerprints taken before — or since! He then took a chemical and, just like that, he got all the black ink off my fingers. When I was wondering how long it would take to wash it off, it was off.

I spoke to him just as I would speak to anybody I was with, and something interesting happened. Apparently he was used to being treated in a very uncooperative manner. When I treated him like a human being he gave me a lecture on fingerprinting and he showed me the charts. It was very interesting. I had really not learned that much about fingerprinting before. People were waiting in line, but I didn't know that until I came out of the room and saw the long line.

Then they took me in to be photographed and hung a number around my neck with a chain. When they were photographing me from the front and side, I remembered all those pictures of wanted people you see in the post office. I remembered how mad they all looked, and I said to myself, "Let me be different." And I smiled as sweetly as I could. There's *one* smiling face somewhere in rogue's gallery!

Then they took me in to be questioned. They actually sat me under a strong light — it's supposed to have a psychological effect on you. But I had already been on television at that time, and I said to myself, "Do they really think this is a strong light? They should see the lights in a television studio!" At *that* time TV lights were not only bright but hot.

They first asked me if I would answer any question, and I said, "Certainly, I will answer your questions. Not because you are law enforcement officers, but because you are fellow human beings, and I answer the questions of all my fellow human beings. Whatever you are in your official capacity, you are first and foremost a human being. And if we could get together as human being to human being we can get done much faster."

And it ended up that way!

They began with the confusing technique. One would fire a question at me. Before I could answer the other would fire a question at me. I had to keep saying, "If you will pardon me for a moment while I answer the other gentleman's question." Then they got down to meaningful questions such as college students ask me. How I warmed up to the subject!

Then they referred to physical violence as being the intent to hurt. They said, "Would you under any circumstances use or sanction the use of physical violence?" I said, "No, this is contrary to God's laws. I would rather have God on my side than any power on earth." I told them the story of the disturbed teenage boy who hit me during our walk together.

Then they said, "Suppose it was necessary for you to defend a loved one?" I said, "Oh, no, I do not believe I could defend a loved one by disobeying Divine Law." I told them about the eight year old girl who had been left in my care and the experience we had with the psychologically sick man who tried to harm her.

Then they got into things very philosophical and said, "If you had to choose between killing and being killed, which would you choose?" I answered, "I don't think I would need to make such a choice — not as long as my life remains in harmony with God's will. Unless, of course, it was my calling to be a martyr. Now, that's a very high calling, it's a very rare calling. I don't believe it's my calling — but the world learns to grow through its martyrs. If I had to make a choice, I would choose to be killed rather than kill."

They said, "Could you give a logical explanation for such an attitude?" Here I was, attempting to explain the attitude of the self-centered nature and the attitude of the God-centered nature so they could understand it! I told them that in my frame of reference I was not the body. I was just wearing the body. *I am that which activates the body* — that's the reality. If I am killed, it destroys merely the clay garment, the body. But if I kill, it injures the reality, the soul!

And they put me down as having a religious basis for my pilgrimage. But suppose I had said, "After all, you've heard of self-defense — why, even the law recognizes self-defense." This might have been considered legal — but not religious.

♫

There was an occasion when I felt that I was indeed battling with the elements. It was my experience of walking through a dust storm which sometimes blew with such force I could scarcely stand against it, while sometimes the dust was so thick I could not see ahead and could only guide myself by the edge of the road. A policeman stopped alongside me, threw open his car door and yelled, "Get in here, woman, before you get killed." I told him I was walking a pilgrimage and did not accept rides (at that time). I also told him that God was my shield and there was nothing to fear. At that moment the winds died down, the dust settled and the sun broke from the clouds. I continued to walk. But the wonderful thing was that I felt spiritually lifted above the hardship.

♫

Concealed in every new situation we face is a spiritual lesson to be learned and a spiritual blessing for us if we learn that lesson. It is good to be tested. We grow and learn through passing tests. I look upon all my tests as good experiences. Before I was tested, I believed I would act in a loving or non-fearing way. *After* I was tested, I knew! Every test turned out to be an uplifting experience. And it is not important that the outcome be according to our wishes.

I remember one experience when it said in the local newspaper I was going to speak at a church service. It showed my picture — front and back, wearing my lettered tunic. A man who belonged to that church was simply horrified to discover that this creature wearing a lettered tunic was about to speak at his church. He called his preacher about it, and he called his friends about it. Somebody told me who he was. I felt so sorry that I had somehow offended a man that I didn't even know. So, I called him!

"This is Peace Pilgrim calling," I said. I could hear him gasp. Afterward he told me that he thought I had called to bawl him out. I said, "I have called to apologize to you because evidently I must have done something to offend you, since without even knowing me you have been apprehensive about my speaking at your church. Therefore I feel I must somehow owe you an apology and I have called to apologize!"

Do you know that man was in tears before the conversation was over? And now we're friends — he corresponded with me afterward. Yes, the law of love works!

☞

Another man once said to me, "I'm surprised at the kind of person you are. After reading your very serious message on the way of peace I expected you to be a very solemn person, but instead I find you bubbling over with joy." I said to him, "Who could know God and not be joyous?"

If you have a long face and a chip on your shoulder, if you are not radiant with joy and friendliness, if you are not filled to overflowing with love and goodwill for all beings and all creatures and all creation, one thing is certain: you do not know God!

Also, life is like a mirror. Smile at it and it smiles back at you. I just put a big smile on my face and everyone smiles back.

If you love people enough, they will respond lovingly. If I offend people, I blame myself, for I know that if my conduct had been correct, they would not have been offended even though they did not agree with me. *Before the tongue can speak, it must have lost the power to wound.*

Let me tell you a time when my love had to be non-verbal. I was trying to help a lady who had been so seriously ill that she could no longer drive her car. She wanted to get to her older sister's house for a few weeks of bed rest so I offered to drive her there. I still had my driver's license at the time. On the way she said, "Peace, I wish you could stay with me for awhile — my older sister is so domineering. I just *dread* being alone with her." I said, "All right, I have a few extra days. I'll stay with you for a little while."

When we were turning into her sister's yard she said, "Peace, I really don't know how my older sister is going to accept you."

She was quite right about her older sister. When her sister took one look at me with my lettered tunic she ordered me out of the house. But it was late at night and she was so afraid of the dark that she said, "Not tonight, you may sleep on the sofa tonight, but the first thing in the morning you must leave!"

Then she hurried her younger sister off to bed way upstairs somewhere. Well, this was worse than I thought it might be. I certainly didn't want to leave my friend in this situation but what could I do? So I looked around to see if there was anything that might permit me to communicate with the older sister. I looked into the kitchen and there was a mountain of dirty dishes and no dishwasher, so I washed all the dishes. Then I cleaned up the kitchen and lay down and slept for a few hours.

In the morning the older sister was in tears and she asked me to stay. She said, "Of course, you understand I was so tired last night I didn't know what I was saying." And we had a wonderful time together before I left them. You see, it just gave me the chance to put my little message into practice. Practice is good; practice makes perfect, they say.

𝒯

During my travels a saloon-keeper called me into his tavern to give me some food, and while I was eating he asked, "How do you feel in a place like this?"

"I know that all human beings are God's children," I replied. "Even when they are not acting that way, I have faith that they could, and I love them for what they could be."

As I rose to leave I noticed a man with a drink in his hand was also on his feet. When he caught my eye he smiled a little, and I smiled at him. "You smiled at me," he said in surprise. "I should think you wouldn't even speak to me but you smiled at me." I smiled again. "I'm not here to judge my fellow human beings," I told him. "I am here to love and serve." Suddenly he was kneeling at my feet and saying, "Everyone else judged me, so I defended myself. You didn't judge me, so now I judge myself. I'm a no-good worthless sinner! I've been squandering my money on liquor. I've been mistreating my family. I've been going from bad to worse!" I put my hand on his shoulder. "You are God's child," I said, "and you could act that way."

He looked with disgust at the drink in his hand, and then hurled it against the bar, shattering the glass. His eyes met mine. "I swear to you I'll never touch that stuff again," he exclaimed. "Never!" And there was a new light in his eyes as he walked through the door with steady steps.

I even know the happy ending to that story. About a year and a half later I heard from a woman in that town. She said as far as anyone knew the man kept his promise. He never touched liquor again. He now has a good job. He is getting along well with his family and has joined a church.

When you approach others in judgment they will be on the defensive. When you are able to approach them in a kindly, loving manner without judgment they will tend to judge themselves and be transformed.

✻

On my pilgrimage a lot of cars stopped and people invited me to ride. Some thought walking meant hitchhiking. I told them I did not cheat God — you don't cheat about counting miles on a pilgrimage.

I remember one day as I walked along the highway a very nice car stopped and the man inside said to me, "How wonderful that you are following your calling!" I replied, "I certainly think that everyone should be doing what he or she feels is the right thing to do."

He then began telling me what he felt motivated toward, and it was a good thing that needed doing. I got quite enthusiastic about it and took it for granted that he was doing it. I said, "That's wonderful! How are you getting along with it?" And he answered,

"Oh, I'm not doing it. That kind of work doesn't *pay* anything."

I shall never forget how desperately unhappy that man was. In this materialistic age we have such a false criteria by which to measure success. We measure it in terms of dollars, in terms of material things. But happiness and inner peace do not lie in that direction. If you know but do not do, you are a very unhappy person indeed.

I had another roadside experience when a fine car stopped with a well-dressed couple inside who began to talk to me. I started to explain to them what I was doing. Suddenly, to my amazement, the man burst into tears. He said, "I have done nothing for peace and you have to do so much!"

And then there was the time when another man stopped his car to talk with me. He looked at me, not unkindly, but with extreme surprise and curiousity, as though he had just glimpsed a live dinosaur. "In this day and age," he exclaimed, "with all the wonderful opportunities the world has to offer, what under the sun made you get out and walk a pilgrimage for peace?"

"In this day and age," I answered, "when humanity totters on the brink of a nuclear war of annihilation, it is not surprising that one life is dedicated to the cause of peace — but rather it is surprising that many lives are not similarly dedicated."

𝄞

When I ended my first cross-country walk I felt so thankful that I had not failed to do what I had been called to do. I either said or thought to myself, "Isn't it wonderful that God can do something through me!"

Afterward I slept at the Grand Central Station railroad terminal in New York City.

When I came into the state between sleep and wakefulness, I had an impression that an indescribably beautiful voice was speaking words of encouragement: *"You are my beloved daughter in whom I am well pleased."* When I came into full wakefulness it seemed as though a celestial orchestra had just finished playing in the station, with its echoes still lingering on. I walked out into the cold morning, but I felt warm. I walked along the cement sidewalk, but I felt I was walking on clouds. The feeling of living in harmony with divine purpose has never left me.

CHAPTER 4:

Reflections on the Pilgrimage

W HEN I FIRST STARTED OUT my tunic read *PEACE PILGRIM* on the front and *Walking Coast to Coast for Peace* on the back. Through the years the message on the back changed from *Walking 10,000 Miles for World Disarmament* to *Walking 25,000 Miles for Peace* and ending with the present message of *25,000 Miles On Foot for Peace.* This walking has taken me several times into the forty-eight states and into Mexico and into all ten Canadian provinces.

I finished counting miles of walking in Washington, D.C. in the fall of 1964. I said to myself, "25,000 miles is enough to count." It kept me tied to the main highways where mileages are recorded on road maps. They're not good places to meet people. They're just good places to count miles. Now I'm free to walk where people are. Also, mileages are not given for my favorite places to walk: beaches, forest paths and mountain trails.

Some things don't seem so difficult, like going without food. I seldom miss more than three to four meals in a row and I never even think about food until it is offered. The most I have gone without food is three days, and then mother nature provided my food — apples that had fallen from a tree. I once fasted as a prayer discipline for 45 days, so I know how long one can go without food! My problem is not how to get enough to eat, it's how to graciously avoid getting too much. Everyone wants to overfeed me!

Going without sleep would be harder, although I can miss one
night's sleep and I don't mind. Every once in awhile I miss a night's
sleep, but not for sometime now. The last time was September of
1977 when I was in a truck stop. I had intended to sleep a little but
it was such a busy truck stop that I spent all night talking to truck
drivers. The first thing after I went in, a truck driver who'd seen
me on television wanted to buy me some food. I sat in a corner
booth. Then truck drivers started to arrive, and it was just one
wave of truck drivers after another that were standing there and
asking me questions, and soforth. I actually talked to them all night
and I never did get to do any sleeping. After awhile somebody
offered me breakfast and I ate that and left.

Another time, a truck driver pulled his truck to the side of the
road and said, "I heard you say over television something about
that endless energy and I just wanted to tell you I had it one time. I
was marooned in a town by a flood. I got so bored that I finally
offered to help and I got interested in getting people out. I worked
without eating, I worked without sleeping, and I wasn't tired . . .
But I don't have it anymore." I said, "Well, what are you working
for now?" "Money," he said. I said, "That should be quite
incidental. You have the endless energy only when you are working
for the good of the whole — you have to stop working for your
little selfish interests."

That's the secret of it. In this world you are given as you give!

♫

I usually average twenty-five miles a day walking, depending
upon how many people stop to talk to me along the way. I have
gone up to fifty miles in one day to keep an appointment or
because there was no shelter available. On very cold nights I walk
through the night to keep warm.

Like the birds, I migrate north in the summer and south in the
winter. If you wish to talk to people out-of-doors you must be
where the weather is pleasant or people will not be out.

Once a six foot fellow, confident he could out walk me, walked
with me for 33 miles. When he gave up, his feet were blistered and
his muscles ached. He was walking on his own strength; I wasn't! I
was walking on that *endless energy* that comes from inner peace.

Another time a woman asked me if she could accompany me

on the pilgrimage. She told me she wanted to get away from "that husband" of hers. Maybe she did have a calling, but her motive was not the highest. Another lady who wished to accompany me for a day could barely walk by afternoon. I sent her home by bus!

I have never experienced any danger on my walks. One time a couple of drunks did follow me in a car, but when I moved off the road they left. Only once has anyone ever thrown something at me: a man in a speeding truck threw a fistful of crumpled dollar bills. I simply gave them to the next church where I spoke.

A college student once asked me if I had ever been mugged. "Mugged?" I answered. "You would have to be a crazy person to mug me — I haven't a penny to my name!"

There was a time when I was walking out of town at sunset and a well-to-do couple in a big house called me over. They had read about my pilgrimage and felt it was their Christian duty to warn me that ahead on the way lay a very wicked place called *'South of the Border.'* They just wanted to warn me not to go near that place. They did not offer food or shelter, however, so I walked on for several hours.

It was a very dark night with a heavy cloud cover and all of a sudden it started to rain. Big drops were coming down, and I was carrying a lot of unanswered mail. I looked for a place where there might be a shelter and nearby I saw a combination gas station, restaurant and motel. I ducked under the roof over the gas pumps and started to put the unanswered mail into the front of my tunic so it wouldn't get wet. The man from the gas station came running out and said, "Don't stand out there in the rain, come into the restaurant." The man in the restaurant said, "Oh, we read all about you, and we would like to offer you a dinner or anything you want." By that time I realized where I was. I was in *'South of the Border.'*

The man from the motel was sitting across the table from me and he gave me a room for the night. They also gave me breakfast the next morning.

There may have been gambling in the back room; something was going on there. But they treated me in a much more Christian fashion than those who warned me against them. It just demonstrates my point that there is good in everybody.

I have received hospitality in the most *unusual* places. These have included a conference table in the Florence, Arizona, city hall and the seat of a fire engine in Tombstone, Arizona. Once I was inadvertently locked for thirteen hours in an icy gas station restroom. My accommodations were quiet and private, although somewhat chilly!

ℐ

I sleep equally well in a soft bed or on the grass beside the road. If I am given food and shelter, fine. If not, I'm just as happy. Many times I am given shelter by total strangers. When hospitality is not available there are always bus depots, railroad stations and all night truck stops.

I remember being offered a queen size bed at a fashionable motel one evening and the next evening space on the concrete floor of a twenty-four hour gasoline station. I slept equally well on both. Several times a friendly sheriff would unlock the door of an unoccupied jail cell.

When no shelter is available to me, I sleep in the fields or by the side of the road with God to guard me.

ℐ

Bridges always offered protection from the elements, as well as dilapidated barns and empty basements of abandoned homes. Culverts and large pipes often served as lodging. But one of my favorite places to sleep is a large haystack piled in an accessible field on a clear night. The stars are my blanket.

Cemeteries are also wonderful places to sleep for the night. They are quiet, the grass is always neatly trimmed, and nobody ever bothers you there. No, there is no intrusion upon the departed spirits. I wish them peace; they understand. But a picnic table at a nearby road stop, a gathering of pine needles in a nearby brush, or the cushion of a blossoming wheat field would serve as well.

One morning, when I was sleeping in a Kansas wheatfield, I was awakened to a very loud noise. I looked up only to see this huge reaper bearing down on me. I immediately rolled over several times to get out of the way of its swirling blades.

I feel a complete protection on my pilgrimage. God is my shield. There are no accidents in the Divine Plan nor does God leave us unattended. No one walks so safely as those who walk humbly and harmlessly with great love and great faith.

I remember a time of the year when it got very cold at night. It went below freezing, but then it warmed up a little in the daytime, so the days were fairly pleasant. It was in the fall, and there were dry leaves on the ground. I was in the middle of the woods and there wasn't a town for miles around. It was sunset and it was a Sunday. Someone had read a thick Sunday newspaper and tossed it beside the road — like they shouldn't, but they do. I picked it up and walked off the road and found a thick evergreen tree. Underneath it was a little depression where some leaves had blown. I pushed a lot of leaves into that depression. Then I put some paper down and placed the rest of the paper over me. When I woke in the morning there was a thick white frost over everything, but the evergreen tree had kept it off of me, and I was snug and warm in my nest of leaves and paper. That's just a tip in case you get caught out some night.

ℐ

Most people interested in vacations are those who are doing things they are not called to do, which they want to get away from for awhile. I couldn't imagine feeling the need of a vacation from my pilgrimage. How good it is to travel south in the fall of the year, experiencing the tranquil beauty of the harvest time — but staying ahead of the frost; experiencing the brilliant beauty of the autumn leaves — but traveling on before they are swept from the trees. How good it is to travel north with the spring, and to enjoy the spring flowers for several months instead of several weeks. I have had both these wonderful experiences in the middle of the country.

During a 1,000 mile walk through New England (which began in Greenwich, Connecticut and ended in Burlington, Vermont) I zig-zagged a lot to walk through not only the large towns but also the smaller towns to which I had been invited. I started among the apple blossoms — I walked among them when they were pink buds, and when their falling petals were as white as falling snow. I ended among the ripened apples, which supplied me with some tasty meals. In between I feasted on luscious wild strawberries and blackberries and blueberries.

Throughout the country I saw much superhighway construction, and I noticed that these super-roads tended to run in the valleys, tunneling through the mountains and sometimes under the rivers. I'm glad that on my pilgrimage I usually followed the old roads that climbed the mountains. What wonderful vistas there were to reward those who attained the summit: sometimes views of towns or roads where I had walked or would walk, sometimes views of valleys covered with fields and orchards. I know that this is an age of efficiency and that superhighways are much more efficient, but I hope there will always be some scenic roads, too. Some roads that climb the mountains.

♬

People sometimes ask me how I spend holidays — especially Christmas. I have spent many of them walking. Many people go for a drive on a holiday, so it is a good time to contact people. I remember one Christmas Eve when I slept out under the stars. One planet was so bright that just a little imagination could transform it into the star of Bethlehem. The next day, at a temperature of 80 degrees, I walked into New Orleans to find poinsettias blooming abundantly for Christmas — and to find some fine, new friends.

I spent one Christmas in Fort Worth, Texas, where the towers and the tall buildings were outlined with colored lights, presenting an unforgettable picture as I walked into the city. That day I was given the welcome present of enough time to catch up with my mail.

People sometimes ask me if I do not feel lonely on holidays. How can I feel lonely when I live in the constant awareness of God's presence? I love and I enjoy being with people, but when I am alone I enjoy being alone with God.

♬

Most of the time in the early years I was offered food and hospitality by people I did not even know. I accept everything as an offering sent from the hand of God. I am equally thankful for the stale bread I received at a migrant worker's home as the sumptuous meal presented to me by a lady friend in the main dining room at the Waldorf Astoria Hotel.

You know, after you have fully surrendered your life to God's will — if it is your calling to go out on faith — you will discover that even the food and shelter you need come to you very easily. Everything, even material things are given. And some amazing things are given that still surprise even me.

I first got to Alaska and Hawaii through a wonderful gift from a wonderful friend. Then some of my friends asked me to consider leading tours there, so I led one to Alaska the summer of 1979 and one to Hawaii the summer of 1980. I arranged the tours to be an educational and inspirational experience for all who participated. We lived simply and traveled light.

I was not idle while in our two newest states. Besides showing my friends around, I did a lot of speaking to groups and over the air. Some of those friends wanted to get an idea of what my pilgrimage life is like, and I think they did. It was a joy to share these inspiring places with them.

I'll tell you another thing that happened: I was figuring out my schedule for North and South Dakota and I knew that in North Dakota I would have to interrupt my schedule to lead the tour in Hawaii. I knew it would be at Bismarck and I knew also that it would take me about a week to hitchhike back from Los Angeles, and I thought, "Oh, a week out of the North Dakota schedule and a week out of the South Dakota schedule. I could really use those two weeks in North and South Dakota." About the time I was thinking these thoughts, someone wrote and offered me air fare to and from Bismarck. It seemed almost like a miracle that it came. And of course this was something that I needed. I do not take anything I do not need, but I did need the time in North and South Dakota. This was a wonderful gift, which I accepted, and for which I shall be eternally grateful.

So even the material things are provided.

I explained to a reporter one time that I just talk to people and after a time they ask me if I want to eat. He pointed out that he had talked to people for months, even years, and they hadn't offered him so much as a sandwich. I told him, "But you're not a peace pilgrim!"

Once a sixteen year old Mexican boy, who had heard me on the radio, raced out as I passed his home and excitedly extended an invitation to stay for the evening. His family lived in a poor itinerant sharecropper's cabin, but I can remember being treated as their honored guest. After a dinner of tortillas and beans, the family rolled up their only rug and placed it as a blanket upon their only bed. In the morning, before departing, they fed me another loving meal of tortillas and beans.

While passing through Memphis, I scampered upon a wooden porch of a one-room house to escape a violent thunderstorm. A black family graciously offered hospitality for the evening. Their warmth was matched by the wood-burning stove that heated their humble home. They shared their meager food of cornbread and water for dinner and breakfast. We all slept on a bare, well-scrubbed floor. I will never forget the genuineness of their hospitality.

One bitter cold morning a college student in Oklahoma gave me the gloves from his hands and threw his scarf around my neck. That night when the temperature had dropped below zero, an Indian couple offered me shelter.

I was once warned not to go to Georgia — and especially not into Albany, Georgia, where fourteen peace walkers were in jail. But I cannot say I found anyone to be really unfriendly. In fact, hospitality was better than average.

The people of minority groups I met took it for granted that I wouldn't discriminate. When they read *Peace Pilgrim* on my tunic, they seemed to trust me. They didn't hesitate to stop and talk. I spoke in a number of minority churches and several of the ministers read my message to their congregations.

♫

Of course, I love everyone I meet. How could I fail to? Within everyone is the spark of God. I am not concerned with racial or ethnic background or the color of one's skin; all people look to me like shining lights! I see in all creatures the reflection of God. All people are my kinfolk — people to me are beautiful!

We people of the world need to find ways to get to know one another — for then we will recognize that our likenesses are so much greater than our differences, however great our differences may seem. Every cell, every human being, is of equal importance and has work to do in this world.

CHAPTER 5:

Living the Simple Life

THE SIMPLIFICATION OF LIFE is one of the steps to inner peace. A persistent simplification will create an inner and outer well-being that places harmony in one's life. For me this began with a discovery of the meaninglessness of possessions beyond my actual and immediate needs. As soon as I had brought myself down to need level, I began to feel a wonderful harmony in my life between inner and outer well-being, between spiritual and material well-being.

Some people seem to think that my life dedicated to simplicity and service is austere and joyless, but they do not know the freedom of simplicity. I am thankful to God every moment of my life for the great riches that have been showered upon me. My life is full and good but never overcrowded. If life is overcrowded then you are doing more than is required for you to do.

My life had been bogged down; I felt greedy before I took my vow of simplicity: *I shall not accept more than I need while others in the world have less than they need.*

You also may have come out of a life where you had too many things. When you have simplified your life, I'm sure you will feel as free as I feel. If your motive is one of giving then you will be given whatever you need.

In my life, what I want and what I need are exactly the same. Anything in excess of needs is burdensome to me. You couldn't give me anything I don't need. I am penniless, but have difficulty remaining so. Several of my well meaning, well-to-do friends have offered me large sums of money, which I of course refused.

I talked to one person who thought I was being deprived of some of the "pleasures" of life. But none of the things I do not use or do not do were taken away from me. I just did not include them when I was choosing a harmonious life. I just had no interest whatsoever in them.

I am not a slave to comfort and convenience. I wouldn't be a pilgrim if I were. We can allow false beliefs to govern our lives and be enslaved by them. Most people do not wish to be free. They would prefer to moan and chafe about how impossible it is to give up their various enslavements to possessions, food, drink, smoking, and so forth. It is not that they can't give them up — they don't really want to give them up.

Our physical needs depend somewhat on the climate in which we live, the state of our health, etc. In general we need a shelter to protect us from the elements; a fire, a blanket, some clothing for warmth; pure air and water and sufficient food for sustenance. There are, of course, needs beyond the physical. These often involve little or no expenditure of money, but this is not always so. For instance, there are some people whose lives are not complete unless they can listen to good music or play some musical instrument. While suggestions may be made as to simple living, simplifying our lives is an individual problem for every one of us.

I learned about forty years ago that money and things wouldn't make people happy. And this has been confirmed many times. I have met many millionaires. They had one thing in common. None of them were happy. Look at Howard Hughes with his 2.5 billion dollars. They say he was the most miserable, fear-ridden creature one could imagine! And I knew a woman who inherited 4.5 million dollars. It ruined her life. Because she was one who had always been a giving person, she wanted to use the money meaningfully. But she discovered it was such a burden to her. She would be better off if she did not have it.

I realize that if you don't have enough you won't be happy.

Neither are you happy if you have too much. It is those who have enough but not too much who are the happiest.

𝒮

I remember a dear lady, who was up in years. She was working so hard and always complaining. I finally said to her, "Why in the world do you need to work so hard when you have only yourself to support?" And she said, "Oh, I have to pay rent on a five room house." "A five room house!" I replied. "But you're alone in the world. Couldn't you live happily in one room?" "Oh yes," she said sadly, "but I have furniture for a five room house." She was actually working her fingers to the bone to provide a proper home for that furniture! And that happens all the time. All I can say is, don't let it happen to you.

Because of our preoccupation with materialism we often miss the best things in life, which are free.

Unnecessary possessions are unnecessary burdens. If you have them, you have to take care of them.

I'll tell you about one more woman. She was liberated, although not in the best possible way. I saw her only occasionally, but I happened to see her about a month after her huge house, in which she and her husband had been living alone since the children were grown, had burned down while they'd been out. They lost everything except the clothes they were wearing. Remembering how attached she had been to that huge house, in spite of the fact that it was such a burden for her to take care of, I started to say a few words of sympathy. But she said, "Don't sympathize with me! Now, you could have the morning after, but not now. Just think, I will never have to clean out that attic. I will never have to clean out those clothes closets. I will never have to clean that basement! Why, I've never felt so free. I just feel I'm starting life all over again!"

She and her husband were living in a sensible size apartment and, indeed, I'm sure they did experience a wonderful sense of freedom. But wouldn't it have been better if they had learned to give and had extended their surplus towards those who needed it? Then they would have been blessed by the giving, and others would have been blessed by the getting. In any case, it was a situation which liberated them.

☾

If you are free, I recommend a hiking trip on a wilderness footpath. How inspiring it is to walk all day in the sunshine and sleep all night under the stars. What a wonderful experience in simple, natural living. Since you carry your food, sleeping equipment, etc., on your back, you learn quickly that unnecessary possessions are unnecessary burdens. You soon realize what the essentials of life are — such as warmth when you are cold, a dry spot on a rainy day, the simplest food when you are hungry, pure cool water when you are thirsty. You soon put material things in their proper place, realizing that they are there for *use*, but relinquishing them when they are not useful. You soon experience and learn to appreciate the great freedom of simplicity.

☾

From May to October of 1952, before the pilgrimage, I walked the 2,000 miles of the Appalachian Trail, from Georgia to Maine, with 500 additional miles for side-trips to points of special beauty.

I lived out-of-doors completely, supplied with only one pair of slacks and shorts, one blouse and sweater, a lightweight blanket, and two double plastic sheets, into which I sometimes stuffed leaves. I was not always completely dry and warm, but I enjoyed it thoroughly. My menu, morning and evening, was two cups of uncooked oatmeal soaked in water and flavored with brown sugar; at noon two cups of double strength dried milk, plus any berries, nuts or greens found in the woods.

I had been thoroughly prepared for my pilgrimage by this toughening process. A walk along the highway seemed easy by comparison.

☾

How good it is to eat fruit tasty and ripe from the tree and vegetables fresh and crisp from the field. And how good it would be for the farming of the future to concentrate on the non-use of poisonous substances, such as sprays, so food would be fit to go from farm to table.

One morning for breakfast I had blueberries covered with dew, picking them from the bushes as I journeyed through the New

England mountains. I thought of my fellow human beings eating various kinds of processed and flavored foods, and I realized that if I could choose my breakfast from all the foods in the world I could not make a better choice than blueberries covered with dew.

In the spring and summer when the days are long, how good it is to get up with the sun and go to bed with the sun. In the fall and winter when the days are shorter you can enjoy some of the night. I am inclined to agree that there is a substance in the air, left there by the sun, which diminishes after the sun goes down and can be absorbed only while you sleep. Sleeping from nine to five is about right for me.

✍

How good it is to work in the invigorating fresh air under the life-giving sun amid the inspiring beauty of nature. There are many who recognize this, like the young man I met whose life had been interrupted by the peacetime draft. While he was away his father, who was in poor health, was not able to keep up the farm and so it was sold. The young man then undertook to do years of distasteful work in order to be able to buy another farm. How good it is to earn your livelihood helping plants to grow to provide people with food. In other words, how good it is to earn your livelihood by contributing constructively to the society in which you live — everyone should, of course, and in a healthy society everyone would.

✍

My clothes are most comfortable as well as most practical. I wear navy blue slacks and a long sleeved shirt topped with my lettered tunic. Along the edge of my tunic, both front and rear, are partitioned compartments which are hemmed up to serve as pockets. These hold all my possessions which consist of a comb, a folding toothbrush, a ballpoint pen, a map, some copies of my message and my mail.

So you can see why I answer my mail faster than most — it keeps my pockets from bulging. My slogan is: *Every ounce counts!* Beneath my outer garments I wear a pair of running shorts and a short sleeved shirt — so I'm always prepared for an invigorating swim if I pass a river or lake.

As I put on my simple clothing one day after a swim in a clear mountain lake I thought of those who have closets full of clothes to take care of, and who carry heavy luggage with them when they travel. I wondered how people would want to so burden themselves, and I felt wonderfully free. This is me and all my possessions. Think of how free I am! If I want to travel, I just stand up and walk away. There is nothing to tie me down.

One outfit of clothing is enough. That's all I've owned since my pilgrimage started in 1953. And I take good care of my things. I can always find a wash basin in a public restroom or a nearby stream to wash my clothes, and drying them is even easier: I just put them on and let the energy from the sun evaporate any dampness.

I wash my skin only with water; soap removes the natural oils. So do the cosmetics and creams most women use.

The only footwear I need is an inexpensive pair of blue sneakers. They have soft fabric tops and soft rubber-like soles. I get them one size too large so I can wiggle my toes. I feel as free as though I were barefoot! And I can usually get 1,500 miles to a pair. I wear a pair of navy blue socks. There's a reason why I chose navy blue for my wearing apparel — it's a very practical color, doesn't show dirt, and the color blue does represent peace and spirituality.

I don't discard any article of wear until it becomes worn to the extent of being unusable. Once when I was about to leave town a hostess said, "Peace, I noticed your shoes were in need of repair, and I would have offered to repair them, but I know so much about sewing that I knew they couldn't be repaired." I said to her, "It's a good thing I know so little about sewing that I didn't know they couldn't be repaired — so I just finished repairing them."

The first few years I used a blue scarf and a blue sweater during chilly weather, but I eventually discarded them as not really essential. I am now so adjustable to changes in temperature that I wear the same clothes summer and winter, indoors and out.

Like the birds, I migrate north in the summer and south in the winter. If you wish to talk to people out-of-doors, you must be where the weather is pleasant or people will not be out.

When the temperature gets high and the sun gets hot there is nothing so welcome as shade. There is a special coolness about the shade of a tree, but unless it is a big tree some shifting is required to stay in the shade. Clouds provide shade as they drift across the sun. A rock provides what I call deep shade; so does a bank early in the morning or late in the afternoon. Sometimes even the shade of a bush is appreciated, or that of a haystack. Man-made things provide shade too. Buildings, of course, and even signs which disfigure the landscape do provide shade. So do bridges, providing shelter from the rain as well. Of course, one can wear a hat or carry an umbrella. I do neither. Once when a reporter asked if by chance I had a folding umbrella in my pockets I replied, ''I won't melt. My skin is waterproof. I don't worry about little discomforts.'' But I've sometimes used a piece of cardboard for a sun shade.

Water is something you think of in hot weather, but I have discovered that if I eat nothing but fruit until my day's walk is over I do not get thirsty. Our physical needs are so simple.

§

After a wonderful sojourn in the wilderness, I remember walking along the streets of a city which had been my home for awhile. It was 1 p.m. Hundreds of neatly dressed human beings with pale or painted faces hurried in rather orderly lines to and from their places of employment. I, in my faded shirt and well-worn slacks, walked among them. The rubber soles of my soft canvas shoes moved noiselessly along beside the clatter of trim, tight shoes with stiltlike heels. In the poorer section I was tolerated. In the wealthier section some glances seemed a bit startled and some were disdainful.

On both sides of us as we walked were displayed the things we can buy if we are willing to stay in the orderly lines day after day, year after year. Some of the things are more or less useful, many are utter trash. Some have a claim to beauty, many are garishly ugly. Thousands of things are displayed — and yet, my friends, the most valuable are missing. Freedom is not displayed, nor health, nor happiness, nor peace of mind. To obtain these things, my friends, you too may need to escape from the orderly lines and risk being looked upon disdainfully.

To the world I may seem very poor, walking penniless and

wearing or carrying in my pockets my only material possessions, but I am really very rich in blessings which no amount of money could buy — health and happiness and inner peace.

The simplified life is a sanctified life,
Much more calm, much less strife.
Oh, what wondrous truths are unveiled —
Projects succeed which had previously failed.
Oh, how beautiful life can be,
Beautiful simplicity.

CHAPTER 6:

Solving Life's Problems

THE PURPOSE OF PROBLEMS is to push you toward obedience to God's laws, which are exact and cannot be changed. We have the free will to obey them or disobey them. Obedience will bring harmony, disobedience will bring you more problems.

Likewise, when societies get out of harmony, problems develop within the society. Collective problems. Their purpose is to push the whole society toward harmony. Individuals can discover that they can not only grow and learn through individual problem solving, they can learn and grow through collective problem solving. I often say I've run out of personal problems, then every once in a while a little one presents itself somewhere. But I hardly recognize it as a problem because it seems so insignificant. Actually, I want to do all my learning and growing now by helping to solve collective problems.

There was a time when I thought it was a nuisance to be confronted with a problem. I tried to get rid of it. I tried to get somebody else to solve it for me. But that time was long ago. It was a great day in my life when I discovered the wonderful purpose of problems. Yes, they have a wonderful purpose.

Some people wish for a life of no problems, but I would never wish such a life for any of you. What I wish for you is the great inner strength to solve your problems meaningfully and grow. Problems are learning and growing experiences. A life without problems would be a barren existence, without the opportunity for spiritual growth.

I once met a woman who had virtually no problems. I was on a late-night radio program in New York City. This woman called the station and wanted me to come to her home. I was intending to spend the night at the bus station, so I said okay. She sent her chauffeur for me, and I found myself in a millionaire's home, talking to a middle-aged woman who seemed like a child. She was so immature, and I wondered at her immaturity, until I realized that the woman had been shielded from all problems by a group of servants and lawyers. She had never come to grips with life. She had not had problems to grow on, and therefore had not grown. Problems are blessings in disguise!

♫

Were I to solve problems for others they would remain stagnant; they would never grow. It would be a great injustice to them. My approach is to help with cause rather than effect. When I help others, it is by instilling within them the inspiration to work out problems by themselves. If you feed a man a meal, you only feed him for a day — but if you teach a man to grow food, you feed him for a lifetime.

It is through solving problems correctly that we grow spiritually. We are never given a burden unless we have the capacity to overcome it. If a great problem is set before you, this merely indicates that you have the great inner strength to solve a great problem. There is never really anything to be discouraged about, because difficulties are opportunities for inner growth, and the greater the difficulty the greater the opportunity for growth.

♫

Difficulties with material things often come to remind us that our concentration should be on spiritual things instead of material things. Sometimes difficulties of the body come to show that the body is just a transient garment, and that the reality is the indestructible essence which activates the body. But when we can say, "Thank God for problems which are sent for our spiritual growth," they are problems no longer. They then become opportunities.

Let me tell you a story of a woman who had a personal

problem. She lived constantly with pain. It was something in her back. I can still see her, arranging the pillows behind her back so it wouldn't hurt quite so much. She was quite bitter about this. I talked to her about the wonderful purpose of problems in our lives, and I tried to inspire her to think about God instead of her problems. I must have been successful to some degree, because one night after she had gone to bed she got to thinking about God.

"God regards me, this little grain of dust, as so important that he sends me just the right problems to grow on," she began thinking. And she turned to God and said, "Oh, dear God, thank you for this pain through which I may grow closer to thee." Then the pain was gone and it has never returned. Perhaps that's what it means when it says: *'In all things be thankful.'* Maybe more often we should pray the prayer of thankfulness for our problems.

Prayer is a concentration of positive thoughts.

♫

Many common problems are caused by wrong attitudes. People see themselves as the center of the universe and judge everything as it relates to them. Naturally you won't be happy that way. You can only be happy when you see things in proper perspective: all human beings are of equal importance in God's sight, and have a job to do in the divine plan.

I'll give you an example of a woman who had some difficulty finding out what her job was in the divine plan. She was in her early forties, single, and needed to earn a living. She hated her work to the extent that it made her sick, and the first thing she did was to go to a psychiatrist who said he would adjust her to her job. So after some adjustment she went back to work. But she still hated her job. She got sick again and then came to me. Well, I asked what her calling was, and she said, "I'm not called to do anything."

That was not true. What she really meant was she didn't know her calling. So I asked her what she *liked* to do because if it is your calling you will do it as easily and joyously as I walk my pilgrimage. I found she liked to do three things. She liked to play the piano, but wasn't good enough to earn her living at that. She liked to swim, but wasn't good enough to be a swimming instructor, and she liked to work with flowers.

I got her a job in a florist shop so she could earn her living working with flowers. She loved it. She said she would do it for nothing. But we used the other things too. Remember, she needed more than just a livelihood. She needed other things. The swimming became her exercise. It fits in with sensible living habits. The piano playing became her path of service. She went to a retirement home and played the old songs for the people there. She got them to sing, and she was good at that. Out of those three things such a beautiful life was built for that woman. She became a very attractive woman and married a year or so later. She stayed right in that life pattern.

∬

I knew another woman who was confined to her room and had been there for quite some time. I went in to see her and I could tell immediately from the lines in her face and the tenseness of her that it wasn't physical at all. And I don't think I had talked to her for more than five minutes before she was telling me all about how mean her sister had been to her. The way she told it, I knew she had told that story again and again and mulled over in her mind constantly that bitterness against her sister. I found myself explaining to her that if she would forgive, ask forgiveness, and make peace with her sister, then she could look for an improvement in her health. "Huh!" she said. "I'd rather die. You have no idea how mean she was." So the situation drifted for awhile.

But early one morning at dawn this woman wrote a beautiful and inspired letter to her sister, which she showed to me. (There is something very wonderful to be said about dawn. Sunset is good, too. The only thing is, at sunset most everybody is awake and they're hurrying and scurrying around. At dawn most everybody is slowed down or asleep and they are much more harmonious when they're asleep. So dawn is often a good time for spiritual things.) I immediately went into town and mailed the letter before she could change her mind. When I got back, she *had* changed her mind — so it's a good thing I had mailed it! She worried a little, but by return mail came a letter from her sister, and her sister was so glad they were to be reconciled. And, you know, on the same day that letter arrived from her sister the woman was up and around and out of bed, and the last I saw of her she was joyously off for a reconciliation with her sister.

There's something to that old saying that hate injures the hater, not the hated.

ℐ

Some people spend much less time picking a life partner than they spend picking out a car. They just drift into these relationships.

No one should enter the family pattern unless one is as much called into it as I was called to my pilgrimage. Otherwise, there will be tragedy. I can remember a woman who couldn't get along with her husband and I could see they didn't have anything in common. I finally said to her, "Why in the world did you marry that man in the first place?" And she said, "All my girlfriends were getting married and he was the best I could do at the time." This happens all the time. Do you wonder why there are so many divorces? People get into the family pattern without being called into it.

Emotional attachment can be a terrible thing. When I was working with people who had problems it often was a problem of some emotional attachment that obviously needed to be broken. One was a sixteen year old girl. By now she is probably happily married to somebody else. I always say time heals all wounds, but she thought then that her heart was broken because her boyfriend had married someone else. Although she had a hard time coming through it, after a time she was able to look upon it philosophically. It does take time. In fact, sometimes people recover quicker from the death of a loved one than from a loved one who has left them.

On the Worry Habit.

Live this day! Yesterday is but a dream and tomorrow is only a vision, but today well-lived makes every yesterday a dream of happiness and every tomorrow a vision of hope. Never agonize over the past or worry over the future. Live this day and live it well.

Worry is a habit. It is something that can be worked on. I call it *relinquishment* of the worry habit. There are techniques that help. I talk to some beautiful church people and I discover they still worry. It's a total waste of time and energy. If you are a praying person who prays with faith, you would immediately, and automatically, take what you're worried about to God in prayer and leave it in God's hands — the best possible hands. This is one technique which is excellent. In the beginning you may have to take it back to God quite a number of times before you develop the habit (which I have developed) of always doing everything you can in a situation, and then leaving the rest safely in God's hands.

How often are you worrying about the present moment? The present is usually all right. If you're worrying, you're either agonizing over the past which you should have forgotten long ago, or else you're apprehensive over the future which hasn't even come yet. We tend to skim right over the *present moment* which is the only moment God gives any of us to live. If you don't live the present moment, you never get around to living at all. And if you do live the present moment, you tend not to worry. For me, every moment is a new and wonderful opportunity to be of service.

On the Anger Habit.

I'll mention here a couple of other habits. One of them is the anger habit. Tremendous energy comes with anger. It's sometimes called the anger energy. Do not suppress it: that would hurt you inside. Do not express it: this would not only hurt you inside, it would cause ripples in your surroundings. What you do is transform it. You somehow use that tremendous energy constructively on a task that needs to be done, or in a beneficial form of exercise.

The best way to talk to you about this is to tell you what some people actually did. For instance, one woman washed all the windows in the house, another woman vacuumed the house whether it needed it or not, and another baked bread — nice, whole grain bread. And another one sat down and played the piano: wild marches at first, then she'd cool down and play gentle things like hymns and lullabies, and then I knew she was all right.

There was a man who got out his manual lawnmower. Remember, the manual lawnmower has no motor. You may never have seen one! And he mowed his big lawn. I was staying next door to him. Then one day he came over and borrowed his neighbor's power lawnmower. I spoke to him about it and he said, "Oh, without the anger energy I could never mow that big lawn with a manual lawnmower." You see, it's really tremendous energy.

Then there was this man who saved his marriage. He had such a bad temper that his young wife was about to leave him and take their two small children along. And he said, "I'm going to do something about this!" And he did. Whenever he felt a temper tantrum coming on, instead of throwing things all over the house which had been his previous custom, he got out there and jogged. Round and round the block, until he was all out of breath and the energy was all gone — and he saved his marriage. It worked. I saw him again years later, and I asked him, "Well, are you still jogging?" "Oh, a little bit for exercise," he said, "but I haven't had a temper tantrum for years." As you use the energy constructively you lose the anger habit.

These techniques have also worked with children. I recall one ten year old boy. I was trying to help his mother because she was having an awful time with him. He got temper tantrums and one time, when he was not having a tantrum, I asked him, "Of all the things you do what takes the most energy?" And he said, "I guess running up the hill in the back of the house." And so we found a wonderful solution. Every time his mother saw the sign of a temper tantrum she would push him out the door and say, "Go run up the hill." It worked so well that when a teacher told me she was having a similar problem with a boy about the same age I suggested she tell him to run around the schoolhouse, and that worked too.

Now I'll tell you about another couple. They got mad at the same time, and they decided to walk around the block. One walked one way and one walked the other way, but they met at frequent intervals. And when they could meet amicably they walked home together and discussed what had caused their angers and what could be done to remedy it in the future. This was a very wise thing to do. You should never try to talk to someone who is angry, because that person is not rational at that time.

I'll tell one more story about a young mother. She has three children under school age and she said, "When I get mad I feel like running, but I can't. I can't leave my three small children. And I usually end up taking it out on them." I said to her, "Have you ever tried running in place?" And I could just see her running in place.

She wrote to me: "Peace, it works wonderfully well. It not only gets rid of the anger energy, but it amuses the children!"

On the Fear Habit.

Fear is also a habit. Fear can be taught and is taught constantly. Fear is perpetuated.

Now, I haven't the slightest fear. God is always with me. But I had a friend who was afraid of a certain ethnic group of people. Her husband had been transferred to another place and she found herself living among this group of people whom she had always feared. I worked with her and first got her acquainted with the music of these people, because she was a musician. Then I found a woman of this particular group who had two children about the same age as my friend's two children, and we went to see her. The two little boys ran off together, the two little girls ran off together, and then we proceeded to get acquainted. Of course, they became fast friends. I remember the time they attended one another's churches. It was a lovely thing. One Sunday they both went to one church and another Sunday they both went to the other church. It was very interesting that when they got to know each other they discovered that their likenesses were much greater than their differences. They came to love each other when they got to know each other.

I knew a lady who was a college English professor. Any time there was the slightest rumble of thunder in the distance she became hysterical. When she was a tiny child, whenever there was a thundershower her mother ran and crawled under the bed and, of course, the kids crawled under with her. She was taught by her mother to fear thundershowers — by example. That's the way children are taught.

Almost all fear is fear of the unknown. Therefore, what's the remedy? *To become acquainted with the thing you fear.* We had to learn all the safety rules before we could become acquainted with thundershowers, but it worked.

I'll tell you another story about fear. I've heard of women who are afraid of mice. And I've personally known women and men who are afraid of dogs. But this woman was afraid of cats. I'm not talking about a wild cat — just common, ordinary household cats.

Now there were cats in her neighborhood. All of her friends had cats. Every time she encountered a cat she screamed, she ran, she became hysterical. She told me she thought every cat she encountered was about to jump at her throat. Now, a psychologist would say, "When she was a baby she was frightened by a cat; she's forgotten that but it still remains in her subconscious." Which might be true. It doesn't matter. I said, "If you wish to lose your fear of cats you must become acquainted with a cat." "Oh no!" she replied. I said, "Well, are you afraid of a kitten?" "Not if it's small enough," she said. So I borrowed a cute, small kitten. They said I could either borrow it or keep it. I brought it to her and I said, "Now are you afraid of that?" "Oh, not that little thing," she said. "All right," I said, "now you must become acquainted. You must feed it, play with it." And of course you know the end of the story. The kitten grew into a cat, but by then she was so attached to it she wouldn't give it up.

✐

Some fears can come from experiences in former lives. In fact the last problem I told about may have had such a source. These are dealt with in the same way. You become acquainted with the things you fear.

There are a few places where you have to use a little different approach. I'll tell you one case where we used the gradual approach. This woman was afraid to sleep in a small room; she would go into a small room, but would not sleep there. This fear did come from a previous life experience. She came for help to where I was working. We put up a cot in the corner of the library (a very large room) for her. She was even afraid to sleep there alone, so I put up another cot and slept there with her the first night. Then when she had learned to at least sleep alone in the library, we put a cot in the dining room, the next smaller room. I slept next to her the first night, and then after that she gradually learned to sleep by herself. Then we tried the biggest bedroom that we had, and so on until she came to the point where she was able to sleep in a small bedroom.

You do not necessarily have to use this gradual method. We did because there are a few kinds of fear that are easier to deal with using the gradual technique. Another one of them is fear of heights, and this also may come from prior experience. Let me tell you, some young, vigorous people have a fear of heights.

What I used to do when people had a fear of heights was to take them to a height where they felt comfortable and really didn't want to go any higher. Then I would stay with them for awhile. I would leave them there with something to read, something to occupy them while they stayed at that height for awhile. The next day we would go immediately to that height and then a little bit higher. Finally they reached the top, accustomed to the height, and no longer had any fear of it.

I have been asked if a certain amount of fear is healthy. I don't think any amount of fear is healthy. Unless you're talking about the fact that if you have fear about a street, you'll look up and down before crossing the street. But you see, I believe we are required to do everything possible for ourselves and therefore when I walk out onto a street I always look up and down. But I don't think that's fear. That's just being sensible. I don't connect that in any way with fear. For instance, I know that if there are little pebbles scattered over a smooth rock, I'm liable to slip if I step on those little pebbles, so I'm careful not to. I'm not afraid, it's just the sensible thing to do.

On Divine Protection.

Recently, while I was leading a group of people on an educational and inspirational tour of four of the Hawaiian Islands, a policeman warned us not to sleep on the beach. It seems there had been a murder on that beach. I was very concerned about all the fear being perpetuated on those beautiful islands. I had no fear. One member of the group tried to tell me about the dangers of the beach. I said to her, "All of us are under the protection of my guardian angel." And we didn't have the slightest incident on any beach.

We were on the beach one night where I think we were the only Anglos. The others were so nice. Several people came up and one said, "A few years back I saw you on television." It must have been five years before, on my first visit to the islands. They even asked for autographs! So I think we should not be apprehensive. I don't think that apprehension can do anything except attract. *"That which I feared came upon me."* I felt perfectly safe on the beach and I felt my whole crowd was protected, and they were.

𝒮

I have a sense of definite protection. Twice I have felt the need to get out of cars I was riding in, and once I saw why. Now, I didn't get out of the car when I was coming down over the "grapevine" into Los Angeles with two high school students. They were seeing how fast they could get the old Chevy to go down hill. I was in the back seat and I felt perfectly all right.

But one time I was with a man who was drinking whisky, and I offered to drive for him. I showed him my driver's license, but he wouldn't let me drive, so I asked him to let me off at the junction. Then I was picked up in a little truck, and we hadn't gone even five miles before we saw the other car. It had gone down into an arroyo and sideswiped a cottonwood tree. On the side where I had been the glass was broken and the roof was bashed in. So at once I saw why I felt the need to get out. The driver wasn't badly hurt. He was cut some but not really hurt.

Another time I did not see any result, but I felt the need to get out. This man was driving recklessly. He would cross over the double center line and pass cars when he couldn't see at all. So I got out. I then got in with a man who was going east at the junction and therefore I never saw what happened to the other car. I don't know. I hope nothing.

So a certain amount of being sensible is good, such as looking up and down a street before you cross, but certainly not the kind of foolish fears many human beings have. You see, if you're going to be fearful — let's say, about sleeping on a beach — you must be terrified every time you sleep in your own home. Look how many people are killed in their own home. Or when you sleep in a hotel room. Look how many people are killed in hotel rooms. This can lead to ridiculous behavior.

I do have a sense of complete protection. If I had felt in any way like I felt in those two cars, I would have taken the whole crowd off the beach. However, I felt absolute protection; I hadn't the slightest apprehension. I knew we were perfectly safe when we stayed on the beach.

𝒮

There are many things we do not fully understand. We just know they happen. For instance, I have been kept from some things that could have hurt me. I was walking down a lane which I knew to be a small lane. The trees met overhead. I could not really see where I was going, but I knew this lane through prior experience, and I could see light at the end of the tunnel. Now I was walking very fast when something, that I can only call a force, stopped me. I mean it was powerful enough to stop me. Then I started ahead very gingerly to see what in the world had happened — and there was a barbed wire stretched across the lane. They were repairing the cattle guard at the end of the lane, which I did not know, and had stretched this wire across to keep the cattle from straying. I would have run into the wire if I had not been stopped. We have much more protection than we realize.

The most significant thing of this kind happened when I was driving a car. I've given up my driver's license now, but all through my driving days I was a good, stable driver, and the car was always under my control. This time I was driving somebody else's car over a road that was not finished yet. Coming down an incline, there was a traffic light at the end of the road where you had to turn either one way or the other. Cars were turning both ways, and turning up on to the road past me. I naturally put my foot on the brake when I saw the light was red, but I had no brakes! I grabbed for the emergency. I had no emergency. I thought if I could put the car into reverse it would stop, although this would tear it to pieces. I attempted to get it into reverse but it wouldn't go. Ahead of me I saw a station wagon with two little children looking out of the back window. I *had* to stop the car! I couldn't turn to the left — there was a rock wall there — and cars were coming up thick and fast. There was a rock wall to the right with a ditch, and my little finite mind said, "Take to the ditch, sideswipe the rock wall. It'll stop the car. It'll tear it up, but it will stop it." *I was not able to do that.* This was the only time in my life when a car was taken out of my control. The car turned to the left, went between two cars, and went up a little dirt road on an incline, which of course stopped the car. I didn't know the dirt road was there. I couldn't possibly see it.

So you see, I've had such amazing things happen to me. You can understand why I feel full of absolute protection. That protection extends even to any group that I am with.

A Helpful Meditation.

I'd like to share this little meditation with you. First, could we agree that God's protection surrounds us? Know that you are God's beautiful child, always in God's hands. Accept God ... accept God's protection ... there is really no problem to fear. Know that you are not the clay garment. Know that you are not the self-centered nature which governs your life needlessly. Know that you are the God-centered nature. The Kingdom of God within. The Indwelling Christ. Eternal and indestructible. Identify with the real you.

> *Peace ... be still ... and know ... that I am God.*
> *Peace ... be still ... and know ... that I am.*
> *Peace ... be still ... and Know.*
> *Peace ... be still.*
> *Peace ... be.*
> *Peace ...*
> > *Peace ...*
> > > *Peace.*

And now, with the knowledge that we are God's perfect children, eternal and indestructible, let us go our separate ways in love, but always remain together in spirit. God bless you and peace to you all.

CHAPTER 7:

Living the Spiritual Life

IN THE BEGINNING I undertook my walking not only to contact people, I undertook it as a prayer discipline to keep me concentrated on my prayer for peace. I hadn't learned yet to pray without ceasing. I also undertook a forty-five day period of prayer and fasting as a prayer discipline.

After the first few years the prayer discipline was completely unnecessary, because I had learned *to pray without ceasing*. I made the contact so thoroughly that into my prayer consciousness I put any condition or person in the world I am concerned about and the rest takes place automatically.

Occasionally some condition is brought back into my conscious mind because I need to really concentrate on it. If some person is in dire difficulty, and that person returns to my mind for thought, I sometimes use the prayer of visualization, which has always been very natural for me, but I understand not so for everybody. I reach out — my divine nature reaches out — to contact their divine nature. Then I have the feeling of lifting them, lifting them, lifting them, and I have the feeling of bringing God's light to them. I try to envision them bathed in God's light, and finally I do see them standing and reaching out their arms bathed in golden light. At that point I leave them in God's hands.

✍

In all people I meet — though some may be governed by the

self-centered nature and may not know their potential at all — I see that divine spark, and that's what I concentrate on. All people look beautiful to me; they look like shining lights to me. I always have the feeling of being thankful for these beautiful people who walk the earth with me.

So I would say part of my prayer is a feeling of thankfulness, and of course a feeling of genuine love for all of God's children and all of God's creation. Prayer is a concentration of positive thoughts. That's a little bit about prayer.

Ways of Prayer.

You can visualize God's light each day and send it to someone who needs help. Your divine nature must reach out and touch the divine nature of another. Within you is the light of the world, it must be shared with the world.

> *Visualize a golden light within you and spread it out. First to those about you — your circle of friends and relatives — and then gradually to the world. Keep on visualizing God's golden light surrounding our earth.*
>
> *And if you have a problem, take the matter to God in prayer, and visualize it in God's hands. Then leave it, knowing it is in the best possible hands, and turn your attention to other things.*

That's not the only prayer you can pray, but I have discovered that for some who were in very great trouble, this prayer of visualization was helpful to them. I've heard of results later, so I do a little of this.

There is also a constant prayer of thankfulness — I am constantly thankful. The world is so beautiful, I am thankful. I have endless energy, I am thankful. I am plugged into the source of Universal Supply, I am thankful. I am plugged into the source of Universal Truth, I am thankful. I have this constant feeling of thankfulness, which is a prayer.

♫

When you're learning, it's true it may be valuable to take special times, even to use special forms . . . I can see that.

Several times people have written to me and said, "Peace, will you pray with me at four o'clock in the afternoon or nine o'clock in the evening, which is such and such a time, daylight saving time?'' I write and tell them, "You don't have to figure all that out for me — plug in at *anytime* and you will be praying with me, and I will be praying with you, because I pray without ceasing."

Ⅱ

Praying without ceasing is not ritualized, nor are there even words. It is a constant state of awareness of oneness with God; it is a sincere seeking for a good thing; and it is a concentration on the thing sought, with faith that it is obtainable. All right prayer has good effect, but if you give your whole life to the prayer you multiply its power... No one really knows the full power of prayer. Of course, there is a relationship between prayer and action. *Receptive prayer* results in an inner receiving, which motivates to right action.

Ⅱ

Let me tell you a story about an answer to prayer. I was picked up late one night by a young policeman as I was walking along a lonely highway. I believe he was thinking in terms of protective custody. He said to me, "Why, nobody in this town would walk out along this highway at this time of night."

I said to him, "Well, you see, I walk completely without fear. Therefore I'm not attracting things which are not good. It says, *That which I feared came upon me.* But I fear nothing and expect only good."

He took me in anyhow, and I found myself in a cell. The floor was littered with old newspapers and cigarette butts and every old thing. The accommodations consisted of a single mattress on the floor and four ragged blankets. There were two women attempting to sleep together on that single mattress. They told me there had been eight women in that cell the night before with those accommodations. There was a rather nice feeling among the prisoners in general. They said to me, "You'll need to have two blankets because you'll be sleeping on the floor." So I took a newspaper and cleared a place on the floor, then put one blanket down and the other blanket over me and slept comfortably enough.

It wasn't the first time I had slept on a cement floor, nor the last. If you're relaxed you can sleep anywhere. When I woke up in the morning I saw this man staring through the bars. I said to him,

"What time does court convene?" He said, "I don't know." I said, "Well, aren't you a policeman?" "No," he said, "I just like to look at the girls." It was one of the town sports. Anyone could come in right off the street and see what they had there today: "Let's go look at the girls!"

One of the women was middle aged and was being held for being drunk and disorderly. It was her seventh offense, she told me, so it wasn't so hard on her. But the other was an eighteen year old girl. She felt her entire life was ruined because of this experience. I said, "It's my second time and I certainly don't think my life is ruined!" I got her all cheered up and we talked about what she'd do when she got out. She was to get out that day or the next day.

Then they changed the guards. I never saw a matron. The new guard saw me and said, "What are you doing in there? I saw your picture in the newspaper. I heard you over the air." Then they just let me go.

But before I left I got a broom from the man who cleaned up around there and gave it to the girls so they could clean up their cell. I also got them a comb; their hair was all matted. They had been there about a week without a comb.

What I really wanted to tell you is that the eighteen year old girl was a deeply religious person. She had been desperately praying for help. I believe that I was picked up off the highway that night and set behind prison bars in answer to her prayers.

☙

The most important part of prayer is what we *feel*, not what we say. We spend a great deal of time telling God what we think should be done, and not enough time waiting in the stillness for God to tell us what to do.

☙

Now, beside God's laws, which are the same for all of us, there is also God's guidance and that is unique for every human soul. If you don't know what God's guidance for your life is, you might try seeking in receptive silence. I used to walk receptive and silent amidst the beauties of nature. Wonderful insights would come to me which I then put into practice in my life.

You might prefer listening to beautiful, uplifting music,

reading a few beautiful words and pondering on them. To me, the beauties of nature were always the most inspiring, and so actually that was my time alone with God. It didn't last more than an hour, if that, and I got so much from it.

Now the young folks talk to me today about things like breathing exercises and meditation techniques, which in some cultures are definitely religious practices. But I say, look what I got from my time alone with God: From the beauty around me, my inspiration; from the silent receptiveness, my meditation; and from my walking, not only my exercise but my breathing. Four things at once! I believe in making very good use of my time. And you can't be too pushy when you're doing four things at once.

Foolish people have sometimes used very strenuous breathing exercises or meditation techniques that tore them apart and pushed them into an undesirable state instead of into the spiritual state. (Yes, that was long before psychedelic drugs!) I always think of the bud of a flower. If you give it proper conditions it will open into a beautiful flower, but if you're impatient and try to tear the petals open you permanently injure the flower for the earth life. The flower can be equated with the earthly human life. Give the spiritual growing-up the proper growing conditions and it will open into a thing of beauty.

𝒥

When you feel the need of a spiritual lift, try getting to bed early and get up early to have a quiet time at dawn. Then carry the serene "in tune" feeling that comes to you into your day, no matter what you may be doing.

𝒥

For those of you who are seeking the spiritual life, I recommend these four daily practices: Spend time alone each day in receptive silence. When angry, or afflicted with any negative emotion, take time to be alone with God. (Do not talk with people who are angry; they are irrational and cannot be reasoned with. If you or they are angry, it is best to leave and pray.) Visualize God's light each day and send it to someone who needs help. Exercise the body, it is the temple of the soul.

𝒥

On Fasting.

I have been asked about my forty-five day period of prayer and fasting. I undertook it as a prayer discipline, to keep me concentrated on my prayer for peace. It was in the second year of my pilgrimage when I was coming slowly back across the country and I wasn't walking extensively.

Fasting can have a great deal of spiritual significance, and though I had already found inner peace, it may have been that the fast helped me to learn to pray without ceasing.

While I fasted I was at the home of a chiropractor who used fasting for healing. He wanted to see how a well person would react to a fast because he had never fasted a well person. I talked to him as a friend; he just observed me, he didn't examine me. (There are many doctors, including medical doctors, who are my friends — but none of them have ever treated me or even examined me. Although occasionally a dentist friend will repair an old cavity which came from my poor eating habits in younger days.) The last meal before my fast was a grapefruit and two oranges, so I wasn't thirsty. The first three days were undertaken without food or water. After that I took distilled water at room temperature. Nothing else. And when I broke my fast it was not unusual — it was the regular way to break a fast. The juice of one freshly squeezed orange every hour the first day. The juice of two freshly squeezed oranges, alternating with the juice of one grapefruit, every two hours the second day. A grapefruit and two oranges three times the third day, and after that adding a little bit until in a week I was able to eat full rations.

It was no different from the usual pattern of fasting. I did obey the laws of fasting: no extreme exertion. I did not walk long distances, though I did walk some. I did some typing for the doctor. I typed until he took the typewriter away about a month along in the fast. He didn't think I ought to handle it anymore, so then I wrote by hand, which was really harder than typing. But I do the best I can with these things.

I didn't go in and talk to his patients as much as I would have liked to because he didn't want me to move around that much. I did go to see them occasionally to help keep up their spirits.

Once during my fast — I remember I was in a state between

wakefulness and sleep — I looked up and saw a dismal cross above me. It was just hanging there, and I knew someone must take up the burden. I reached up to accept it and I was immediately lifted above the cross where all was light and beauty. All that was needed was the willingness to accept the burden — and then I was raised above it. Instead of hardships, I found a wonderful sense of peace and joy.

On Healing.

One must be very careful when praying for others to pray for the removal of the *cause* and not the removal of the symptom. A simple healing prayer is this:

> *"Bring this life into harmony with Divine Purpose . . . may this life come into harmony with God's Will. May you so live that all who meet you will be uplifted, that all who bless you will be blessed, that all who serve you will receive the greatest satisfaction. If any should attempt to harm you, may they contact your thought of God and be healed."*

Eager beaver psychic healers are those who work on the removal of symptoms and not the removal of cause. When you desire phenomena, you possess phenomena; you do not get God. Let's say I am a psychic healer living next door to you, and you have chosen to come into this life to face some kind of physical symptom until you have removed the cause. Well, when the symptom manifests, I remove it. And so the symptom manifests again, and I then remove it again, and I manage to keep that symptom removed.

When you step over to the disembodied side of life, for another reason altogether, instead of blessing me for having removed the symptom you'll say, "That meddler! I came to solve this problem but she kept removing the symptom and therefore I never solved it!"

That's what I mean when I speak about some who are content to deal with the removal of symptoms. When one meddles in the life of another it will just cause the symptoms not only to re-manifest, but carry over into another lifetime. Most healers do not know this and they go on merrily removing symptoms.

I admit that a long time ago, before I really knew what I was doing, when working with people who had problems I comforted them by putting my hands on the back of their neck and the forehead. I certainly wouldn't do that now. I did not realize I was doing anything but to comfort. Now I place any problem into my prayer consciousness. I place it into the best possible hands — God's hands, and turn my attention to other things.

The Power of Thought.

Are you a slave to your self-centered nature, or does your divine nature guide your life? Do you know that every moment of your life you're creating through thought? You create your own inner condition; you're helping create the conditions around you.

Christian teachings tell us that *'As a man thinketh in his heart, so is he.'* Which is saying very clearly that we are creating the conditions around us. If we could look a bit more deeply into life, we might see that physical difficulties are reflections of spiritual difficulties, and that negative thoughts and feelings are much more harmful than disease germs.

If you realized how powerful your thoughts are, you would never think a defeatest or negative thought. Since we create through thought, we need to concentrate very strongly on positive thoughts. If you think you can't do something, you can't. But if you think you can, you may be surprised to discover that you can. It is important that our thoughts be constantly for the best that could happen in a situation — for the good things we would like to see happen.

I have met some 'new age' people who had heard some prediction of disaster and were actually concentrating on that. What a terrible thing to do! Why, we're creating every moment of our lives through thought. And we're helping to create the conditions around us.

When you hear of any predictions of disaster there's a reason for it. The reason is that you are to throw the entire weight of your positive thought in the opposite direction.

For instance, when there were dozens of predictions that half of California was to slide into the sea from a terrible earthquake, I deliberately planned to be in that section of California. There wasn't a tremor. But I missed some of my friends who were on the east coast, playing it safe.

⚘

Remember where it says there shall be prophecies and they shall fail? Why is it? Because all you can predict is the *trend* of things. You can never say what the outcome will be, because we are constantly able to turn that prediction in another direction, in a positive direction if we get together on that.

⚘

Every good thing you do, every good thing you say, every good thought you think, vibrates on and on and never ceases. The evil remains only until it is overcome by the good, but the good remains forever.

⚘

Just concentrate on thinking and living and acting in harmony with God's laws and inspiring others to do likewise.

Every time you meet a person, think of some encouraging thing to say — a kind word, a helpful suggestion, an expression of admiration. Never think of any right effort as being fruitless. All right effort bears fruit, whether we see the results or not.

⚘

Be a sweet melody in the great orchestration, instead of a discordant note. The medicine this sick world needs is love. Hatred must be replaced by love, and fear by faith that love will prevail.

⚘

A song has this phrase: *Love is flowing like a river, flowing out from you and me. Spreading out into the desert, setting all the captives free.*

Yes, the captives are those who don't know who they are, those who don't know they are God's children.

⚘

Remember this: *Be still and know that I am God.* Don't ever forget who you are! You cannot be where God is not.

⚘

The Change Called Death.

Life is a series of tests, but if you pass your tests you'll look back upon them as good experiences. I look back on all of my tests as good experiences, including the night I faced death in a blinding snowstorm. It was the first year of my pilgrimage and the most beautiful experience I ever had.

I was walking in a very isolated section of the high mountains of Arizona where there was no human habitation for many miles. That afternoon there came a surprising snowstorm, out of season. I have never seen such a storm. If the snow had been rain you would have called it a cloudburst. Never had I seen snow dumped down like that!

All of a sudden I was walking in deep snow and was unable to see through what was falling. Suddenly I realized that the cars had stopped running. I supposed they were getting stuck on the highway and unable to pass. Then it got dark. There must have been a heavy cloud cover. I could not see my hand before my face, and the snow was blowing into my face and closing my eyes. It was getting cold. It was the kind of cold that penetrates into the marrow of the bone.

If ever I were to lose faith and feel fear, this would have been the time, because I knew there was no human help at hand. Instead, the whole experience of the cold and the snow and the darkness seemed unreal. Only God seemed real . . . nothing else. I made a complete identification — not with my body, the clay garment which is destructible — but with the reality which activates the body and is indestructible.

I felt so free; I felt that everything would be all right, whether I remained to serve in this earth life or if I went on to serve in another freer life beyond. I felt guided to keep on walking, and I did, even though I couldn't tell whether I was walking along the highway or out into some field. I couldn't see anything. My feet in my low canvas shoes were like lumps of ice. They felt so heavy as I plodded along. My body began to turn numb with cold.

After there was more numbness than pain, there came what some would call an hallucination — and what some would call a vision. It was as though I became aware, not only of the embodied side of life where everything was black darkness, bitter cold and swirling snow — but also so close it seemed I could step right into it, of the *unembodied* side of life where everything was warmth and light. There was such great beauty. It began with familiar color, but transcended familiar color. It began with familiar music, but transcended familiar music.

Then I saw beings. They were very far away. One of them moved toward me very quickly. When she came close enough, I recognized her. She looked much younger than she had looked when she passed over.

I believe that at the time of the beginning of the change called death, those nearest and dearest come to welcome us. I have been with dying friends who have stepped over and I remember well how they talked to their loved ones on both sides . . . as though they were all right there in the room together.

So I thought my time had come to step over, and I greeted her. I either said or thought, "You have come for me?" But she shook her head! She motioned for me to go back! And just at that exact moment I ran into the railing of a bridge. The vision was gone.

Because I felt guided to do so, I groped my way down that snowy embankment and got under the bridge. There I found a large cardboard packing box with wrapping paper in it. Very slowly and clumsily in my numb condition, I managed to get myself into that packing box, and somehow with my numbed fingers managed to pull the wrapping paper around me. There under the bridge, during the snowstorm, I slept. Even there shelter had been provided — but provided also was this experience.

Had you looked at me in the midst of the snowstorm, you might have said, "What a terrible experience that poor woman is going through." But looking back on it I can only say: What a wonderful experience in which I faced death, feeling not fear, but the constant awareness of the presence of God, which is what you take right over with you.

I believe I had the great privilege of experiencing the beginning of the change called death. So now I can rejoice with my loved ones as they make the glorious transition to a freer living. I can look forward to the change called death as life's last great adventure.

◊

I have been asked what I mean when I've said I had started the process we call death. Of course, the change called death is a process. First you begin to perceive not only this side of life, but the unembodied side of life. Then you begin to recognize loved ones on the unembodied side as they move toward you, and you find you can communicate with both sides. That's as far as I went. Next comes the breaking of the "silver cord" — and then communication with those on this side is cut off, although you can still see and hear them. You find yourself in the "common meeting place" with your unembodied loved ones for a wondrous reunion, and later you go to the level where you are to learn, and also to serve, if you are far enough advanced.

The unembodied side of life is *right here in another dimension.* The two worlds intermingle. We are aware of our world but they are aware of both worlds — usually. Some communication is possible; for instance, we can pray for them and they can pray for us.

ℐ

Death is a beautiful liberation into a freer life. The limiting clay garment, the body, is put aside. The self-centered nature goes with you to learn and grow on the disembodied side of life, and then returns here into a suitable clay garment and suitable circumstances to learn the lessons we need to learn. Could we but see a bit deeper into life, we would grieve at birth and rejoice at death. If we but knew how short is the earth life in comparison with the whole, we would be less troubled with the difficulties of the earth life than we are troubled now with the difficulties of one of our days.

ℐ

The memorial service should be a joyous farewell party, recalling the good the person has done, reading favorite poems and singing favorite songs. If we did this, the liberated one would be rejoicing with us.

ℐ

As I accepted the change of the golden hair of my childhood to the reddish-brown hair of my youth without regret, so I also accept my silver hair — and I am ready to accept the time when my hair and the rest of my clay garment returns to the dust from which it came, while my spirit goes on to freer living. It is the season for my hair to be silver, and each season has its lessons to teach. Each season of life is wonderful if you have learned the lessons of the season before. It is only when you go on with lessons unlearned that you wish for a return.

On Religion.

Religion is not an end in itself. One's union with God is the ultimate goal. There are so many religions because immature people tend to emphasize trivial differences instead of important likenesses. Differences between faiths lie in creeds and rituals rather than religious principles.

How diverse the many paths seem to be at times, but do they not all come together eventually upon the same mountaintop? Are they not all striving for the same thing?

If you are guided toward a faith, use it as a stepping stone to God, not as a barrier between yourself and God's other children or as a tower to hold you aloft from others. If you are not guided toward a faith (or even if you are) seek God in the silence — seek within.

When we attempt to isolate another we only isolate ourselves. We are all God's children and there are no favorites. God is revealed to all who seek; God speaks to all who will listen. Be still and know God.

ℐ

I am a deeply religious person, but I belong to no denomination. I follow the spirit of God's law, not the letter of the law. One can become so attached to the outward symbols and structure of religion that one forgets its original intent — to bring one closer to God. We can only gain access to the Kingdom of God by realizing it dwells within us as well as in all humanity. Know that we are all cells in the ocean of infinity, each contributing to the others' welfare.

ℐ

I read the King James version of the New Testament in its entirety and some excerpts from the Old Testament just after the beginning of my pilgrimage. They are important books to a great number of people, and I felt the need to inquire of their contents in order to make my outreach to others more complete. Yes, the Bible contains a great many truths, but most often these truths are not really understood. People replace the spirit of the law with the letter of the law and truth becomes distorted into falsehood. If you desire confirmation of a truth, it is best to seek it from *within* and not upon a printed page.

You will note that Jesus says, "Why do you call me 'Lord, Lord' and do not what I say?" He expresses this thought more than once. Therefore, it seems to me that a real Christian would be living by the laws of God that Jesus taught. Jesus also says, "Say not, 'Lo here' or 'Lo there', for behold, the Kingdom of God is within you." In so many illustrations he tells people what they are capable of. Real Christians would allow their lives to be governed by the Kingdom of God within — by the God-centered nature — which is sometimes called the *indwelling Christ*.

∬

Many people profess Christianity. Very few live it — almost none. And when you live it people may think you're crazy. It has been truthfully said that the world is equally shocked by one who repudiates Christianity and by one who practices it.

I believe Jesus would accept me because I do what he told people to do. This doesn't mean, though, that all who call themselves Christian would accept me. Of course I love and appreciate Jesus and I wish Christians would learn to obey his commandments. It would be a most wonderful world.

The Way of Love.

Evil cannot be overcome by more evil. Evil can only be overcome by good. It is the lesson of the way of love. The contest in the world today is between the old way of attempting to overcome evil with evil, which with modern weapons would lead to complete chaos, and the way of overcoming evil with good, which would lead to a glorious and mature life.

We need not reach out to tear down that which is evil because nothing which is contrary to God's laws can endure. All not-good things in the world are transient, containing within themselves the seeds of their own destruction. We can help them to fade away more quickly only insofar as we remain in obedience to God's law that evil must be overcome with good. Those who create something which is evil in order to overcome something else which is evil only double the evil.

God's laws are implemented constantly, for everything out of harmony is on its way out. How can anyone doubt that eventually God will prevail? It is only *how soon* that is up to us. And with how much violence they will pass away is also up to us. Insofar as we are willing to let them go, there will be less violence — insofar as we have been able to build the new within the old, there will be less violence; so let us work on that. Let us help the phoenix to rise from the ashes, let us help lay the foundation for a new renaissance, let us help to accelerate the spiritual awakening until it lifts us into the golden age which would come!

In order to help usher in the golden age we must see the good in people. We must know it is there, no matter how deeply it may be buried. Yes, apathy is there and selfishness is there — but good is there also. It is not through judgment that the good can be reached, but through love and faith.

Pure love is a willingness to give, without a thought of receiving anything in return. Love can save the world from nuclear destruction. *Love God:* turn to God with receptiveness and responsiveness. *Love your fellow human beings:* turn to them with friendliness and givingness. Make yourself fit to be called a child of God by living the way of love.

Do you know God? Do you know there is a power greater than ourselves which manifests itself within us as well as everywhere else in the universe? This I call God. Do you know what it is to know God, to have God's constant guidance, a constant awareness of God's presence? To know God is to reflect love toward all people and all creations. To know God is to feel peace within — a calmness, a serenity, an unshakeableness which enables you to face any situation. To know God is to be so filled with joy that it bubbles over and goes forth to bless the world.

I have only one desire now: to do God's will for me. There is no conflict. When God guides me to walk a pilgrimage I do it gladly.

When God guides me to do other things I do them just as gladly. If what I do brings criticism upon me I take it with head unbowed. If what I do brings me praise I pass it immediately along to God, for I am only the instrument through which God does the work. When God guides me to do something I am given strength, I am given supply, I am shown the way. I am given the words to speak. Whether the path is easy or hard I walk in the light of God's love and peace and joy, and I turn to God with psalms of thanksgiving and praise. This it is to know God. And knowing God is not reserved for the great ones. It is for little folks like you and me. God is always seeking you — every one of you.

You can find God if you will only seek — by obeying divine laws, by loving people, by relinquishing self-will, attachments, negative thoughts and feelings. And when you find God it will be in the stillness. You will find God within.

Thoughts to Ponder

photographed by Carla Anette

Thoughts to Ponder

THERE IS NO GLIMPSE OF THE LIGHT without walking the path. You can't get it from anyone else, nor can you give it to anyone. Just take whatever steps seem easiest for you, and as you take a few steps it will be easier for you to take a few more.

∅

When you know your part in the scheme of things, in the Divine Plan, there is never a feeling of inadequacy. You are always given the resources for any situation, any obstacle. There is no strain; there is always security.

∅

When you have constant communion with God, a constant receiving from within, there is never any doubt; you know your way. You become an instrument through which a job is done, therefore you have no feeling of self-achievement.

∅

The spiritual life is the real life; all else is illusion and deception. Only those who are attached to God alone are truly free. Only those who live up to the highest light live in harmony. All who act upon their highest motivations become a power for good. It is not important that others be noticeably affected: results should never be sought or desired. Know that every right thing you do — every good word you say — every positive thought you think — has good effect.

"This is me and all my earthly possessions. Think of how free I am. If I want to travel, I just stand up and walk away."

Few find inner peace but this is not because they try and fail, it is because they do not try.

ℐ

There is nothing that happens by chance in our universe. Everything unfolds according to higher laws — everything is regulated by divine order.

ℐ

Judging others will avail you nothing and injure you spiritually. Only if you can inspire others to judge themselves will anything worthwhile have been accomplished.

ℐ

I perceived the entirely self-centered life as not worth living. If what you're doing will not benefit others besides yourself, it is not worth doing.

ℐ

The Godly way is one of the few simple precepts that even a child can understand. Truth is simple — it's just not so simple to live it. Therefore, immature people tend to hide behind complicated interpretations in order to avoid living simple truth.

ℐ

Humanity has only scratched the surface of its real potential. Anyone can plug into the Divine Current by discovering the truth of Jesus and other prophets who taught that *the Kingdom of God is Within.*

ℐ

If you want to teach people, young or old, you must start where they are: at their level of understanding — and use words they understand. When you have captured their attention, you can take them as far as they are able to go. If you perceive that they are already beyond your level of understanding, let them teach you. Since steps toward spiritual advancement are taken in such a varied order, most of us can teach one another.

ℐ

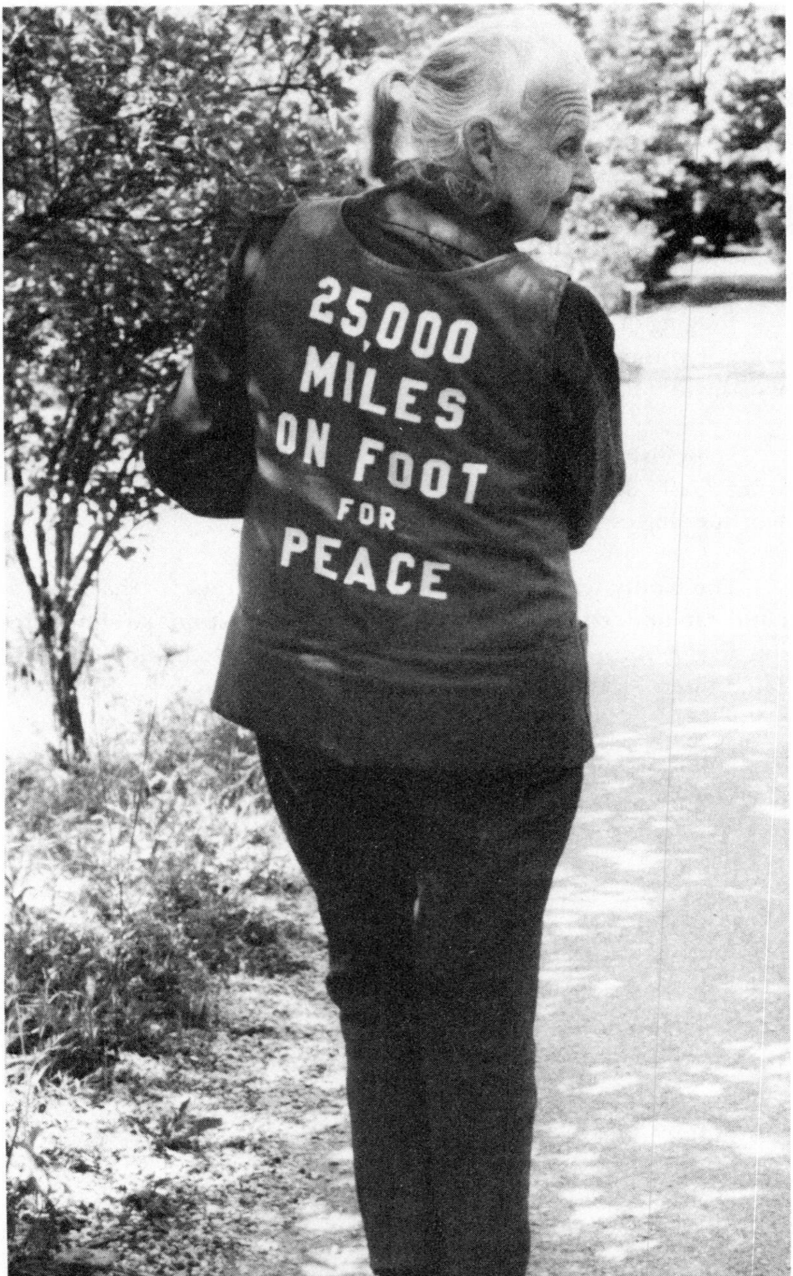
25,000
MILES
ON FOOT
FOR
PEACE

Life is a mixture of successes and failures. May you be encouraged by the successes and strengthened by the failures. As long as you never lose faith in God, you will be victorious over any situation you may face.

_ℐ_

When you look at things emotionally, you will not see them clearly; when you perceive things spiritually, you will understand.

_ℐ_

Live in the present. Do the things that need to be done. Do all the good you can each day. The future will unfold.

_ℐ_

There are many lessons to be learned and scales to be balanced. The laws of the universe cannot be altered for one's convenience. Humanity must learn to accept everything that life offers as a learning experience. It is for this reason spiritually immature people cannot be spoon-fed by someone else. The seeker must walk alone — with God.

_ℐ_

If you give your life as a prayer, you intensify the prayer beyond all measure.

_ℐ_

Although others may feel sorry for you, _never_ feel sorry for yourself: it has a deadly effect on spiritual well-being. Recognize all problems, no matter how difficult, as opportunities for spiritual growth, and make the most of these opportunities.

_ℐ_

To attain inner peace you must actually give your life, not just your possessions. When you at last give your life — bringing into alignment your beliefs and the way you live — then, and only then, can you begin to find inner peace.

_ℐ_

photo by Martin Beck, courtesy J. and A. Rush

CHAPTER 8:

The Way of Peace

T HIS IS THE WAY OF PEACE: *Overcome evil with good, falsehood with truth, and hatred with love.*

It is hard for people to understand that all war is bad and self-defeating. People in their immaturity attempt to overcome evil with more evil, and that multiplies the evil. Only good can overcome evil.

My simple peace message is adequate — really just the message that the way of peace is the way of love. Love is the greatest power on earth. It conquers all things. One in harmony with God's law of love has more strength than an army, for one need not subdue an adversary; an adversary can be transformed.

One day as I was walking along the highway I began to sing peace words to a familiar tune which I believe sums up the present world situation in a nutshell:

> *The world is feverishly working to build the things of war,*
> *The world is preparing destruction of a kind unknown before.*
> *I hear much cursing of enemies, and arguments increase,*
> *But, oh, the world is longing, is yearning,*
> *Is praying for peace — for peace!*

The nuclear bomb says to us: "Make peace or perish!" We recognize that we can no longer think in terms of military victory, that a nuclear war would mean mutual annihilation. Many face this critical situation with apathy, some with frustration, but only a very few face it constructively.

There is such a great need for constructive peace action. We live at a crisis period in human affairs, and those of us who are living today face a very momentous decision: A choice between nuclear war of annihilation and a golden age of peace. All who are living today will help to make this choice, for the tide of world affairs now drifts in the direction of war and destruction. So all who do nothing in this crisis situation are choosing to let it drift. Those who wish to choose peace must *act meaningfully* for peace. And become a part of the stirring and awakening which has begun and is accelerating. And help to accelerate it sufficiently to turn the tide. In this crisis situation peace is certainly everybody's business! The time to work for peace is *now*.

Ultimate peace begins within; when we find peace within there will be no more conflict, no more occasion for war. If this is the peace you seek, purify your body by sensible living habits, purify your mind by expelling all negative thoughts, purify your motives by casting out any ideas of greed or self-striving and by seeking to serve your fellow human beings, purify your desires by eliminating all wishes for material possessions or self-glorification and by desiring to know and do God's will for you. Inspire others to do likewise.

Some will prefer to work on an interim peace — a setting up of mechanisms to resolve conflicts in a world where conflicts still exist — so that although there may still be psychological violence there will no longer be physical violence. If this is the peace you seek, work on a world scale for world disarmament and reconstruction, for a world government which will include all people, for world thinking: placing the welfare of the human family above the welfare of any nation. Work on a national scale for changing the function of the so-called Defense Department from destruction to construction. So much constructive work is needed among the less fortunate peoples in the world, and for the adjustment of our economy to a peacetime situation. Lots of problems to solve here. Get others to work with you.

ᔕ

We can work on inner peace and world peace at the same time.

On one hand, people have found inner peace by losing themselves in a cause larger than themselves, like the cause of world peace, because finding inner peace means coming from the self-centered life into the life centered in the good of the whole. On the other hand, one of the ways of working for world peace is to work for more inner peace, because world peace will never be stable until enough of us find inner peace to stabilize it.

ℐ

My inner peace remains in spite of any outward thing. Only insofar as I remain in harmony can I draw others into harmony, and so much more harmony is needed before the world can find peace. This doesn't mean that I am not concerned about world happenings. A time like this calls for much peace prayer and peace effort. All right work and all right prayer has effect, all good effort bears good fruit, whether we see the results or not. In spite of the darkness in the present world situation I am not discouraged. I know that just as human life proceeds toward harmony through a series of hills and valleys, so a society has its ups and downs in its search for peace.

There is within the hearts of people deep desire for peace on earth, and they would speak for peace if they were not bound by apathy, by ignorance, by fear. It is the job of the peacemakers to inspire them from their apathy, to dispel their ignorance with truth, to allay their fear with faith that God's laws work — and work for good.

Knowing that all things contrary to God's laws are transient, let us avoid despair and radiate hope for a warless world. Peace is possible, for thoughts have tremendous power.

A few really dedicated people can offset the ill effects of masses of out-of-harmony people, so we who work for peace must not falter. We must continue to pray for peace and to act for peace in whatever way we can, we must continue to speak for peace and to live the way of peace; to inspire others, we must continue to think of peace and to know that peace is possible. What we dwell upon we help to bring into manifestation. One little person, giving all of her time to peace, makes news. Many people, giving some of their time, can make history.

ℐ

One day a lady said to me, "Peace, I'm praying with you for peace, but of course I don't believe it's possible." I said, "Don't you believe peace is God's will?" "Oh, yes," she said, "I know it is." I said, "How can you tell me that which is God's will is impossible? It's not only possible, it's inevitable, but how *soon* is up to us."

♫

Never underestimate the power of a loosely knit group working for a good cause. All of us who work for peace together, all of us who pray for peace together, are a small minority, but a powerful spiritual fellowship. Our power is beyond our numbers.

Those who seem to fail pave the way and often contribute more than those who finally succeed. I cannot help feeling grateful to the peace pioneers, who worked for peace when the going was rough and there were no apparent results.

♫

One of the most common questions asked of me is: "Have you seen any results from your pilgrimage?" The answer is that I've never asked to see results — I leave the results in God's hands. They may not even be manifest in my lifetime, but eventually they will become manifest. And, believe it or not, I have seen results: Lots of letters from people indicating they have been inspired to do something for peace in their own way — anything from writing letters to Congress to making peace with some friend or relation. And it all adds up.

Now, as I look back at the overall efforts of all the peacemakers, I can see the results. When I began my pilgrimage, people accepted war as a necessary part of life. Now, the peacemakers are on the popular side! When I started out, there was very little interest in the inner search. I could actually make an inquiry at a state college and discover that two-thirds to three-quarters of the students at that time considered themselves agnostic if not atheist. Now, I can hardly find a student or a person who isn't interested in the deepest kind of searching. To me that is the most hopeful sign of all.

♫

On the one hand it can be said: *How tragic that our material advancement has gotten so far ahead of our spiritual advancement that we stand on the brink of destroying all life on earth.* On the other hand it can be said: *How good that we finally realize that military victory is impossible, so that immature people and even not-good people now have an incentive to lay down their arms.* Both statements are true.

𝄞

There is no greater block to world peace, or inner peace than fear. It has led us to manufacture implements of mass destruction. What we fear we tend to develop an unreasonable hatred for — so we come to hate and fear. This not only injures us psychologically and aggravates world tensions, but through such negative concentration we tend to attract the things which we fear. If we fear nothing and radiate love, we can expect good things to come. How much this world needs the message and the example of love and faith!

𝄞

Peace and freedom! These things shall be! How soon these things shall be — whether now or whether after great destruction and new beginnings and eons of time — is up to us!

𝄞

Much research and experimentation needs to be done on peaceful ways of resolving conflicts. We can work as groups, or as an individual right where we are, undertaking specific peace projects, commending and strengthening the good wherever we find it.

𝄞

You can only expect to change one nation — your own. After your nation has changed itself, the example may inspire other nations to change themselves. If any influential nation had the great spiritual strength to lay down its arms and appear with clean hands before the world, the world would be changed. I see no evidence that any influential nation has such great spiritual strength and courage. Therefore disarmament will be a slow process, motivated by the wish to survive.

𝄞

The darkness that we see in our world today is due to the disintegration of things out of harmony with God's laws. The basic conflict is not between nations, it is between two opposing beliefs.

The first is that evil can be overcome by more evil, that the end justifies the means. This belief is very prevalent in our world today. It is the *war way*. It is the official position of every major nation.

Then there is the way that was taught two thousand years ago — of overcoming evil with good, which is my way, the way Jesus taught. Never loose faith: God's way is bound to prevail in the end.

ℐ

In order for the world to become peaceful, people must become more peaceful. Among mature people war would not be a problem — it would be impossible. In their immaturity people want, at the same time, peace and the things which make war. However, people can mature just as children grow up. Yes, our institutions and our leaders reflect our immaturity, but as we mature we will elect better leaders and set up better institutions. It always comes back to the thing so many of us wish to avoid: working to improve ourselves.

The sanctuary of peace dwells within. Seek it out and all things will be added to you. We're coming closer and closer to the time when enough of us will have found inner peace to affect our institutions for the better. And as soon as this happens the institutions will in turn, through example, affect for the better those who are still immature.

ℐ

Peace will probably come to the world in the same way as it has come to our land. Out of the chaos of civil war, Indian wars and the duels of hundreds of years ago, has come order. Mechanisms have been set up to avoid physical violence, while psychological violence still endures. The smaller units, the states, have given up to the larger unit, the United States, the right to make war. Yes, I think the time will come when the smaller units, the nations, will give up to the larger unit, the United Nations, one single right: the right to make war.

I don't believe the nations would or should give up other rights. People have the most control over their affairs at a grass-roots level. Anything that can be fairly and efficiently handled at a grass-roots level should be thus handled, and only delegated to a higher authority when necessary.

The United Nations would have as its job maintaining a peaceful situation in the world. As long as we remain immature the UN would have a police force to deal with individual offenders against the peace of the world — by removing them, I would hope, for their rehabilitation. Also it should have an unarmed peace force to deal with war prevention. While our nation can deal with problems like an inadequate food supply, the UN would have to deal with problems like a country striving for freedom — and freedom is now the desire of all human hearts.

I once said to a woman who believed in war and Christian values: "On the one hand you talk about Christian values, on the other hand you say, 'Isn't force the only deterrent they respect?' This has been our trouble down through the ages — we have given only lip service to Christian values, and lived by the jungle law of tooth and claw. We have quoted *'Be not overcome of evil, overcome evil with good'* and then attempted to overcome evil with more evil, thereby multiplying the evil. We worship God, but have no faith in the working of God's laws of love. The world awaits the *living* of the law of love, which will reach the divine within all human beings and transform them."

The pastor of a large Canadian church, who had recently returned from a visit to the Orient, told me that the Buddhists are sending two thousand missionaries to convert the Christians to the way of non-violence!

During World War II, an American Sunday School teacher who was in the Pacific had captured a Japanese soldier. In marching the soldier to camp, the American discovered that his prisoner spoke English. "You know what," said the Japanese soldier. "I was once a Christian." The American deliberated a moment and then said, "Why did you give up Christianity?" A look of surprise came upon the Japanese soldier, and he answered with a puzzled expression, "How can I be a soldier and still be a Christian?"

What people do not realize is that nonviolence can be applied in all situations, including World War II. I met four of the Danish people who used the way of nonviolence and love in World War II, and it was a wonderful story.

Now, when the Germans occupied France, the French would often kill the German soldier who was patrolling, and then the Germans would wipe out the whole block in retaliation. When the Germans marched into Denmark, the Danish people began a program of non-cooperation. You know, they say the way to a man's heart is through his stomach — many Danish people actually used that way. They would say to the German soldier who was patrolling, "As a representative of the Nazi Government, you have no right to be here anymore than we would have the right to be in your land, but you are also a young man far from home. Maybe you're homesick, and if you as a fellow human being would like to take off your gun belt and come in and share our evening meal with us, you are welcome." It usually didn't take more than one try. After that the German soldier would get to thinking, "Gee, these are nice people. What are we doing here?"

The Danes also used nonviolent ways to protect the Jewish people in Denmark.

ℐ

I met a Jewish woman who had been married and living with her parents in Germany under Hitler at the time of World War II. She was married when she was sixteen. Her first child was born when she was seventeen and the second when she was eighteen. She was nineteen when three things happened to her. The first: her home was destroyed and her parents killed by an English bomb. I guess they thought they were liberating her. The second thing that happened: her husband was taken away by the Nazis, and she assumed he was dead because she never heard from him again. The third thing that happened: she was injured and her two small children were killed by an American bomb. When I saw her she still carried the effects of the injury. Again, we were 'liberating' her.

In her injured condition she wandered round and round with the refugees. Sometimes extenuating circumstances make you take a spiritual leap. She began thinking, *They have injured and even destroyed our bodies, but they have injured their own souls, and that is worse*. She was able to feel compassion and pray for all connected with the situation, the killed and the killer. She was able to maintain such a good attitude that she was befriended by German people, who at the risk of their lives, got her to England where she was befriended by the English people, and eventually got to the United States.

Now obviously this represents the most amazing victory of the spirit under the most difficult circumstances you could possibly imagine. It also illustrates something else. Who or what was that woman's enemy? Was it the English who destroyed her home and killed her parents, or the Germans who killed her husband, or the Americans who injured her and killed her two small children? The answer is amazingly obvious: it was *war* that was her real enemy. It was the false belief that violence will accomplish something, that evil can be overcome by more evil. *That* was her real enemy, and it's the real enemy of all mankind.

☙

Just as a human soul that faces great difficulties also faces great opportunities for spiritual growth, so a human society that faces destruction also faces the opportunity to enter a period of renaissance. I think that, barring an accident, the wish to survive will keep us from a nuclear war. And I think both sides will change. We will move toward more economic and social democracy, and they will move toward more political and individual democracy. The ideal society has yet to be built — one which balances nicely collective well-being and individual well-being.

Stories about Non-Violence.

One day as I was musing beside an old fort, I wondered what it would say to the people of the world if it could speak, and I wrote this article:

AN OLD FORT SPEAKS

When I was built much time and money was spent on me, because it was thought that I would defend the city against all invaders. Now I stand forlorn, since it does not require great wisdom to recognize that I am obsolete. But I am not the only material defense which is obsolete. Even the most modern of them are obsolete now, although you in your fear and your bewilderment still cling to them. But while in your immaturity you lavish your time and your treasure upon them, you know in your hearts that they cannot defend you against anything. You know that you stand, seemingly defenseless, facing a new age, while the nuclear bomb says to you, "Make peace or perish!" But are you really defenseless because all material defenses have crumbled as they were bound to crumble? Have you forgotten the defense which cannot crumble, the defense which lies in obedience to higher law? Down through the ages your best teachings and your best selves have been telling you that evil can only be overcome by good, and experience has shown that if you want to make friends you must be friendly. When will you have wisdom enough to forsake the path to annihilation and turn to the defense which is timeless and ageless and changeless? People of earth, the decision is before you! You can still choose life, but you must choose quickly!

THIS STRANGE CREATURE CALLED MAN

An outsider might view this strange creature called Man this way:

A Being from another world parked his space ship in an isolated spot. The next morning he passed a military camp, where he saw men sticking knives fastened to odd looking poles into bags of straw. "What is this?" he asked a uniformed youth. "Bayonet practice," answered the youth. "We're practicing on dummies. We have to learn to use the bayonet a certain way to kill a man. Of course we don't kill many men with bayonets. We kill most of them with bombs." "But why should you want to learn to kill men?" exclaimed the Being, aghast. "We don't," said the youth bitterly. "We are sent here against our will and we don't know what to do about it."

That afternoon the being passed through a large city. He noticed a crowd gathered in a public square to see a uniformed youth being decorated with a medal. "Why is he being decorated with a medal?" inquired the Being. "Because he killed a hundred men in battle," said the man beside him. The Being looked with horror upon the youth who had killed a hundred men and walked away.

In another part of the city the Being heard a radio announcing loudly that a certain man was soon to be executed. "Why is he to be put to death?" asked the Being. "Because he killed two men," said the man beside him. The Being walked away bewildered.

That evening, after the Being had thought the matter over, he opened his notebook and wrote: *It seems that all youths are forced to learn how to kill men efficiently. Those who succeed in killing a large number of men are rewarded with medals. Those who turn out to be poor killers and succeed in killing only a few men are punished by being put to death.*

The Being shook his head sadly and added a postscript: *It looks as though this strange creature called Man will exterminate himself very quickly.*

A Vision of Hope for Peace.

At the end of my forty-five day period of prayer and fasting, as I lay between sleeping and waking, a wonderful vision came to me . . . a vision of hope. I saw the nations of the world arming for war. I spoke to them, but they would not listen. I wept for them, but they paid no attention. I prayed for them, and then as I looked about me I saw that the people of the world were praying with me. Next I noticed that a luminous mist was rising above us as we prayed, and it gradually took form. A radiant figure emerged whose white robes were full of light and whose face was so bright I could scarcely look upon it. When the figure spoke the gentle voice had the power of thunder. "Put up your swords!" the figure said. "Those who take the sword shall perish by the sword!" And the nations of the world looked up startled and dropped their armaments, and the people of the world rejoiced together.

More Thoughts on Peace and Disarmament.

I would like to emphasize again that right prayer leads to right action, that "faith without works is dead." An excellent way to put thoughts into action is to write a letter for peace.

J

Disarmament is slow in materializing — partly because fear is so prevalent, partly because there are vain hopes that arms might still accomplish some desired objective, partly because some economies seem to be functioning rather profitably in a situation of war preparation.

ℐ

The new age demands higher values. Those who spoke of peace were once called idealists, but in this nuclear age the idealists have become the only realists. We have always thought of ourselves as having high ideals. Let us apply some of them in this crisis situation.

ℐ

Believing that war is contrary to the will of God and to common sense, and feeling that the way of peace is the way of love, I shall work for peace by using the way of love myself, by helping any group I am a part of to use it, by helping the nation of which I am a citizen to use it, by helping the United Nations to use it, and by praying that the way of love be used all over the world.

ℐ

I would say to the military: yes, we need to be defended; yes, we need you. The Air Force can clean up the air, the Marines can take care of the despoiled forests, the Navy can clean the oceans, the Coast Guard can take care of the rivers, and the Army can be used to build adequate drainage projects to prevent disastrous floods, and other such benefits for mankind.

ℐ

We limit ourselves by thinking that things can't be done. Many think peace in the world is impossible — many think that inner peace cannot be attained. It's the one who doesn't know it can't be done who does it!

ℐ

The basic cause of all our difficulties is immaturity. That's why I talk so much about peace within ourselves as a step toward peace in our world. If we were mature, war would not be possible and peace would be assured. In our immaturity we do not know the laws of the universe, and we think evil can be overcome by more evil. One symptom of our immaturity is greed, making it difficult for us to learn the simple lesson of sharing . . .

Now, I realize that sometimes the symptoms become so acute that if we don't work on them we might not survive to work on the cause, so during the war in Vietnam I did participate in some peaceable peace demonstrations. That was an amazing time. The people of this country stopped the war in Vietnam, in spite of the government. It just shows the power of the people of this country.

Then there are symptoms of symptoms, like extensive starvation. I would like to give everyone access to pure food, pure water, and pure air. I would like to be able to supply all their material needs, and also give them access to good food for thought, and beautiful surroundings and all things that inspire. You don't have to be very good at arithmetic to figure out that if the nations of the world would stop manufacturing implements of destruction, the conditions for a very good life could be provided for all people.

We must walk according to the highest light we have, encountering lovingly those who are out of harmony, and trying to inspire them toward a better way. Whenever you bring harmony into any unpeaceful situation, you contribute to the cause of peace. When you do something for world peace, peace among groups, peace among individuals, or your own inner peace, you improve the total peace picture.

We must never forget that disobedience to God's laws brings disaster, although people eventually do learn by their own mistakes.

Now let's look at our world. A poor, war-weary world. What's the matter with us? We're so way off on the material side: even if we do not have it we desire it. We are so lacking on the spiritual side: whenever we discover all the technological advances, the first thing we do is to turn them into weapons and use them to kill people. This is because our spiritual well-being lags so far behind. The valid research for the future is on the spiritual side. We need to bring the two into balance so we'll know how to use well the material well-being we already have.

During the war in Vietnam there was intense peace activity. When the war was finished there was a letdown and a period of apathy resulted. I suppose this was inevitable. It happens after every war.

After every war there is also a period of violence. I saw it after both World War I and World War II. I remember after World War II a man in Camden, New Jersey had just killed five people on the street, and when they grabbed him he said, "You taught me to kill." He was taught by the military. The man who shot from the University of Texas tower and killed fifteen people and wounded others was taught by the military during the Vietnam War.

The Price of Peace.

We seem always ready to pay the price for war. Almost gladly we give our time and our treasure — our limbs and even our lives — for war. But we expect to get peace for nothing. We expect to be able to flagrantly disobey God's laws and get peace as a result. Well, we *won't* get peace for nothing — and we won't get peace by disobeying the laws of God. We'll get peace only when we are willing to pay the *price* of peace. And to a world drunk with power, corrupted by greed, deluded by false prophets, the price of peace may seem high indeed. For the price of peace is obedience to the higher laws: evil can only be overcome by good and hatred by love; only a good means can attain a good end.

The price of peace is to abandon fear and replace it with faith — faith that if we obey God's laws we will receive God's blessings. The price of peace is to abandon hate and allow love to reign supreme in our hearts — love for all our fellow human beings over the world. The price of peace is to abandon arrogance and replace it with repentance and humility, remembering that the way of peace is the way of love. The price of peace is to abandon greed and replace it with giving, so that none will be spiritually injured by having more than they need while others in the world still have less than they need.

People of the world, the time for decision is short. It is measured in a few years. The choice is ours as to whether or not we will pay the price of peace. If we are not willing to pay it, all that we hold dear will be consumed in the flame of war. The darkness in our world today is due to the disintegration of things which are contrary to God's laws. Let us never say hopelessly this is the darkness before a storm; rather let us say with faith this is the darkness before the dawn of the golden age of peace, which we cannot now even imagine. For this, let us hope and work and pray.

CHAPTER 9:

Extensions of Pacifism

MANY PEOPLE KNOW the simple spiritual law that evil can only be overcome by good. Pacifists not only know it, they also attempt to live it. In their attempt to live it they refuse to use or sanction the use of physical violence. Those who oppose war but would use physical violence in their personal lives I would call *war resisters* but not pacifists. Those who use the non-violent method only because they believe it to be the most effective method I would call *nonviolent resisters* but not pacifists. Pacifists use the nonviolent way because they believe it to be the right way, and under no circumstances would they use or sanction the use of any other way.

The animal nature thinks in terms of using 'the jungle law of tooth and claw' to eliminate all opposition. But this law solves no problems for humans; it can only postpone solutions, and in the long run it worsens things.

Some nations, even while they are using the jungle law in their dealings with other nations — while they are at war — recognize that pacifists cannot act that way and exempt them from military service. Instead they usually either serve in non-military ways or spend time in prison. They are often called conscientious objectors. There are, of course, very few conscientious objectors, because very few have attained sufficient inner awakening at such an early age.

When I talk about extensions of pacifism, I realize that I am speaking just to fellow pacifists, a very small group in any modern society. With this small group, a group that I admire and respect very much, I would like to discuss three extensions of pacifism that I have made.

I have extended my pacifism to include non-use of psychological violence as well as non-use of physical violence. Therefore I no longer become angry. I not only do not say angry words, I do not even think angry thoughts! If someone does an unkind thing to me, I feel only compassion instead of resentment. Even upon those who cause suffering I look with deep compassion, knowing the harvest of sorrow that lies in store for them. If there were those who hated me, I would love them in return, knowing that hatred can only be overcome by love, and knowing that there is good in all human beings which can be reached by a loving approach. Those who use the non-violent method without love may have difficulty. If you force people to do things your way without helping to transform them, the problem is not really solved. If you can remember that *we are not really separate from one another* it may increase your wish to transform instead of subdue. And to extend your pacifism to include non-use of psychological violence as well as non-use of physical violence.

I wouldn't recommend civil disobedience except as a last resort. In general, people can accomplish much more out of jail than they can behind bars. Nor would I encourage any threatening action that advocates psychological violence as a solution to problem solving. What is done to a single person affects us all.

I have extended pacifism to include non-payment for war as well as non-participation in war. Therefore I no longer knowingly pay federal taxes. For more than forty-three years I have lived below income tax level. I admit, of course, that there is a second reason for this: I cannot accept more than I need while others in the world have less than they need. Naturally I have never paid taxes on liquor or tobacco because I have never used these items, but I also don't pay luxury tax because I don't use luxury items and I don't pay amusement tax because I don't patronize amusements.

Now, the federal government may be supporting some things we approve of, but unfortunately it is not presently possible to pay for them and not for war. A pacifist would answer *no* were the federal government to say, "If you will spend half of your time on war activities you may spend the other half of your time on good works." Yet there are pacifists who answer *yes* when it is a question of money instead of time. I realize that human beings tend to be inconsistent in one way or another, but since I feel I must be as consistent as I know how to be I have extended my pacifism to include non-payment for war as well as non-participation in war.

I have extended my pacifism to include non-harming of creatures as well as non-harming of human beings. Therefore for many years I have not eaten flesh — not meat, fowl, or fish. I also don't use furs or feathers, leather or bone. I realize that some people are vegetarians merely for health reasons, and are not necessarily opposed to war. Some people may miss the eating of flesh, but I do not. I don't crave animal flesh any more than the average person craves human flesh. I think most pacifists — in fact, most modern human beings — would not eat flesh if they had to kill the creatures themselves. I think if you were to visit a slaughterhouse it might encourage you to extend your pacifism to include non-harming of creatures as well as non-harming of human beings.

There is an awakening taking place today which may very well develop into a new renaissance. Perhaps the wish to survive is pushing us this way . . . perhaps it is the realization that something must be done about our present plight that motivates us. Groups that have traditionally used violence are talking about nonviolent resistance. People who have participated enthusiastically in war activities are becoming war resisters. An ever increasing number of people are becoming pacifists. I am, therefore, expecting the pacifists to move forward also and make some extensions of their pacifism.

𝒮

The following quotations were among the few notes that Peace Pilgrim carried in the pockets of her tunic:

General Omar Bradley: "Wars can be prevented just as surely as they can be provoked, and we who fail to prevent them must share in the guilt for the dead."

General Douglas MacArthur: "I have known war as few men now living know it. Its very destructiveness on both friend and foe has rendered it useless as a means of settling international disputes."

Pope John XXIII: "If civil authorities legislate for or allow anything that is contrary to the will of God, neither the laws made nor the authorizations granted can be binding on the consciences of the citizens, since God has more right to be obeyed than men."

Dwight D. Eisenhower: "Every gun that is made, every warship launched, every rocket fired, signifies in the final sense a theft from those who are hungry and are not fed, those who are cold and not clothed." Speaking "as one who has witnessed the horror and lingering sadness of war — as one who knows that another war could utterly destroy this civilization," he warned against the military-industrial complex.

John F. Kennedy: "Mankind must put an end to war, or war will put an end to mankind . . . War will exist until that distant day when the conscientious objector enjoys the same reputation and prestige that the warrior does today."

Lyndon B. Johnson: "The guns and the bombs, the rockets and the warships, all are symbols of human failure."

Pope John Paul II: "In the face of the man-made calamity that every war is, one must affirm and reaffirm, again and again, that the waging of war is *not* inevitable or unchangeable. Humanity is not destined to self-destruction. Clashes of ideologies, aspirations and needs can and must be settled and resolved by means other than war and violence."

Herman Goering, at the Nuremburg Trials: "Why, of course people don't want war. Why should some poor slob on a farm want to risk his life in a war when the best he can get out of it is to come back to his farm in one piece? Naturally the common people don't want war: neither in Russia, nor in England, nor for that matter in Germany. That is understood. But after all, it is the leaders of a country who determine the policy, and it is always a simple matter to drag the people along, whether it is a democracy, or a fascist dictatorship, or a parliament, or a communist dictatorship. Voice or no voice, the people can always be brought to the bidding of the leaders. That is easy. All you have to do is tell them they are being attacked, and denounce the pacifists for lack of patriotism and exposing the country to danger. It works the same in any country."

ॐ

I have never met anyone who built a bomb shelter and felt protected by it. I have never met a modern military man who did not realize that military victory is a concept which became obsolete with the coming of the nuclear age, and most civilians realize this also. Wisdom demands that we stop preparing to wage a war which would eliminate mankind — and start preparing to eliminate the *seeds* of war.

CHAPTER 10:

Children and the Way of Peace

I MET A COUPLE WHO WERE DETERMINED that they were going to train their four children in the way of peace. Every night at dinner they gave a regular sermon on peace. But one evening I heard the father scream at the older son. The next evening I heard the older son scream at the younger son in the same tone of voice. What the parents said hadn't made any impression at all — what they *did* was what the children were following.

Implanting spiritual ideas in children is very important. Many people live their entire lives according to the concepts that are implanted in them in childhood. When children learn they will get the most attention and love through doing constructive things, they will tend to stop doing destructive things. Most important of all, remember that children learn through example. No matter what you say, it is what you *do* that will have an influence on them.

This is a very challenging area for parents. Are you training your children in the way of love which is the way of the future?

§

It concerns me when I see a small child watching the hero shoot the villain on television. It is teaching the small child to believe that shooting people is heroic. The hero just did it and it was effective. It was acceptable and the hero was well thought of afterward.

If enough of us find inner peace to affect the institution of television, the little child will see the hero transform the villain and

117

bring him to a good life. He'll see the hero do something significant to serve fellow human beings. So little children will get the idea that if you want to be a hero you must help people.

𝒥

A minister I know spent some time in Russia. He saw no Russian children playing with guns. He visited the large toy stores in Moscow, and discovered that there were no toy guns or other toy implements of destruction for sale.

Peaceful training is given in a few small cultures right within our larger culture. I knew a couple who lived for ten or twelve years among the Hopi Indians. They said to me, "Peace, this is amazing — they never hurt anyone."

I have walked among the Amish people myself. They have sizable communities. Peaceful, secure communities with no violence. I talked to them and I realized it's because they learn, as little children onward, that it would be unthinkable to harm a human being. Therefore they never do it. This can be accomplished if you are brought up that way.

𝒥

Once a woman brought her four or five year old daughter over to me and said, "Peace, will you explain to my daughter what is good and what is bad?" I said to the child, "Bad is something that hurts somebody. When you eat junk food that hurts you, so that is bad." She understood. "Good is something that helps somebody. When you pick up your toys and put them back into your toy box that helps your mother, so that is good." She understood. Sometimes the simplest explanation is best.

𝒥

When my folks put me to bed they would say to me very wisely, "It gets dark so that it will be restful for you to sleep. Now go to sleep in the nice friendly, restful darkness." And so to me darkness has always seemed to be friendly and restful. And when I'm either walking all night to keep warm or sleeping beside the road, there I am, in the nice, friendly restful darkness.

𝒥

Children need roots somewhere while they are growing up, and parents might do well to choose the place where they want to raise them before they have them.

CHAPTER 11:

Transforming Our Society

I HAVE BEEN ASKED if I have any ideas for peaceful solutions to some of our world and national problems. For one, I think a very long stride toward world peace would be the establishment of a world language.

I first ran into the language barrier in Spanish-speaking Mexico, where I could speak to people only through my translated message and my smile. Then in the Province of Quebec in Canada I ran into it again. Canada is a bilingual country. The schools in Quebec are conducted in French, and many of the people in Quebec cannot speak English. I had a translated message, and I was offered food and shelter through sign language. But there the communication just about ended. It made me realize anew the great need for a world language.

I think a committee of experts appointed by the United Nations should decide as quickly as possible what language would be best. Once a world language is decided upon it can be taught in all the schools along with the national language, so that very soon every literate person in the world can talk to every other literate person in the world. I think this would be the biggest single step we could take toward world understanding, and a long stride toward world peace. When we can talk together we will realize that our likenesses are so much greater than our differences, however great our differences may seem.

On Democracy and Society.

I define democracy as control by the people. Slaves are those who allow others to control their lives. Insofar as people succeed in solving their problems fairly and efficiently at a grassroots level, they retain control over their lives. Insofar as they delegate their problem solving to a higher authority, they lose control over their lives.

We have a goodly amount of individual democracy — for example, the right of a minority of one to continue to speak. And we have a lot of political democracy. We are making progress on *social* democracy. If we had social democracy every human being would be evaluated according to merit, not according to groups. We've legislated in that direction; we need to go a long way still, but we're getting there.

Where we fall the shortest is in economic democracy. Here we have not too much control and I'm concerned about this. Remember, if we want to set a good example to the world we must improve ourselves. I'll tell you a sad story:

I was walking through someone's living room. Two comedians on television were making jokes before a live audience and one of them said, "I got a medal from my company." "Why?" "I found a way to make their product wear out quicker!" And everybody in that live audience laughed.

This is no laughing matter. Raw materials are in short supply; energy is running out. Future generations will look upon us as idiots for manufacturing for obsolescence. Yes, everybody knows what we are doing and they even laugh about it. This needs to be remedied, obviously.

The other thing that needs to be remedied is unemployment. I am terribly concerned about it. Some seven or eight million of our fellow human beings in this country are unemployed. And what does that do to people? They deteriorate psychologically because they are being told by society that they are not needed, that there is no place for them. Unemployment is a terrible thing. We need to remedy this and we need to remedy it immediately.

I would suggest that after a certain length of time all employable unemployed could apply for community work, funded as welfare is funded. The work wouldn't even need to be full time, but they would be earning what they received.

There is no psychologically well person who does not wish to be meaningfully occupied with something. I understand there are a few psychologically sick people — especially those who have been unemployed for a long time and have terribly deteriorated. But this is not true of most people. Most people would actually jump at the chance to be able to do something.

ℐ

From a spiritual point of view, the best way to cope with anything that is out of harmony, such as communism as it is practiced today, is never to fear it — that gives it power. Bring good influences to bear upon it; make yourself a good example. Never try to overcome it by adopting its false philosophy. For instance, part of the philosophy of communist governments is said to be *'The end justifies the means'* — which is actually the philosophy of all countries that use war as a means. Rather, adopt the spiritual philosophy of *'The means determine the end,'* and remember only a good means can really attain a good end.

ℐ

We can only change through example. Therefore, if I had the power to do so in this country I would set a very gentle, good example. I would establish a Peace Department in our government. It would have very useful work to do. It would research peaceful ways of resolving conflicts, war prevention measures and economic adjustments to peace. It would be established with some fanfare and we would ask every other nation to establish similar departments and come and work with us for peace. I think many nations would be willing to do so. Communications among the Peace Departments would be a step toward peace in our world.

ℐ

During the war in Vietnam I asked my correspondents from all over the world the same question: "What country do your fellow countrymen consider to be the biggest menace to the peace of the world?" The answer was unanimous. It wasn't Russia and it wasn't China. It was us! I asked, *"Why?"* The answers varied a bit. The Orientals answered, "Because you are the only nation that used the nuclear bomb to kill people, and there is no evidence that you might not do so again." In South America and Latin America they tended to say, "It's Vietnam today — it will be us tomorrow." In Europe and some other places the answer tended to be, "Your economy works most smoothly in a war or war preparation period," or, "In your country there is big money to be made on war or war preparation."

I don't like to report this, it's a negative thing, but I do think we need to see that the countries of the world do not always see our kind heart when they look across the sea. Instead they are apprehensive about our actions.

⌀

I would like to see us not only take all the steps we can in the direction of disarmament and peace in the world, I would also like to see us set a better and better example in the world.

Within the last couple of years a number of my foreign friends have said to me, "Russia signed Salt II, why didn't you sign it? Are you less interested in disarmament than the Russians?" I couldn't answer them. I wish we had signed it. It was a gentle step, not nearly enough, but we should have signed it, then worked hard for Salt III and every agreement that we could get.

⌀

On my pilgrimage across Canada I was invited to speak during the Youth Choir Concert of the Union of Spiritual Communities of Christ, commonly known as Doukhobors, a pacifist group which migrated from Russia in the last century. I said to them, "You have a special message to this world, specifically in Russia. Since many of you speak Russian, why not send a mission of peace to Russia? This choir, for example? You have a unique opportunity to talk to them in their own language, moreso than the usual delegation that often cannot communicate with them. This sort of exchange is necessary in the present historical crisis."

⌀

The United Nations needs to be improved. We people of the world need to learn to put the welfare of the whole human family above the welfare of any group. Starvation and suffering needs to be alleviated. An extensive exchange of people among the nations of the world would be very helpful.

There are some national problems in connection with peace —

work needs to be done on peace among groups. Our number one national problem, however, is the adjustment of our economy to a peacetime situation.

Community Peace Action.

In this crisis period there should be a community peace committee in every town. Such a group can begin with a handful of concerned people.

I have been suggesting that Community Peace Fellowships start with a *Peace Prayer Group* for seeking the way of peace. At the first meeting consider inner peace. Pray about it and discuss it. If you become aware of some inner block which is hampering your spiritual progress, concentrate between meetings on removing that block. At the second meeting consider harmony among individuals. If you realize that you are out of harmony with some person, do something between meetings to remedy this. At the third meeting consider harmony among groups. Between meetings try to do something as a group to show friendliness toward or to help some other group. At the fourth meeting consider peace among nations. Take action between meetings by commending someone who has done something good for peace. At the next meeting, start all over again.

In some places my literature has been used for their prayer groups, since it deals with peace from a spiritual viewpoint. Read a paragraph, dwell on it in receptive silence, then talk about it. Have as many prayer meetings as you need to get through the literature. Anyone who can understand and feel the spiritual truths contained therein is spiritually ready to work for peace.

Then would come a *Peace Study Group*. We need to get a clear picture of what the present world situation is like and what will be needful to convert it into a peaceful world situation. Certainly all present wars must cease. Obviously we need to find a way to lay down our arms together. We need to set up mechanisms to avoid *physical* violence in the world where psychological violence still exists.

After world problems and steps toward their solution become pretty clear to you, you and your friends are ready to become a *Peace Action Group*. You can become a Peace Action Group gradually, acting upon any problem that you have learned to understand. Peace action should always take the form of living the way of peace. It can also take the form of letter-writing: to legislators about peace legislation you are interested in, to editors on peace subjects, to friends on what you have learned about peace. It can take the form of public meetings with speakers on peace subjects, distributing peace literature, talking to people about peace, a peace week, a peace fair, a peace walk, a peace parade, or a peace float. It can take the form of voting for those who are committed to the way of peace.

You have much more power when you are working *for* the right thing than when you are working against the wrong thing. And, of course, if the right thing is established wrong things will fade away of their own accord. Grass-roots peace work is vitally important. All who work for peace belong to a special peace fellowship — whether we work together or apart.

✠

Some of the steps toward peace that I talked about when I started out have now been taken or at least begun. An extensive people-to-people approach is well under way, with student exchanges and cultural exchanges. Research on peaceful ways of resolving conflicts is now being done at a number of our colleges, and courses are being taught also by our neighbor, Canada.

✠

I believe it is quite possible for us to obtain an outer peace at the present time. Historically speaking, when human beings are faced with the choice between destruction and change, they are apt to choose change, and it's about the only thing that will make them choose change. So we have the possibility at the present time to take a different direction in the world — the possibility exists!

✠

Little people of the world, let us never feel helpless again. Let us remember that if enough of us ask together even very big things like world disarmament and world peace will be granted. *Let's ask together!*

CHAPTER 12:

The Way of a Pilgrim

ONCE I WAS ASKED, "What do peace pilgrims do?" A peace pilgrim prays and works for peace within and without. A peace pilgrim accepts the way of love as the way of peace, and to depart from the way of love is to depart from the way of a peace pilgrim. A peace pilgrim obeys God's laws and seeks God's guidance for one's life by being receptively silent. A peace pilgrim faces life squarely, solves its problems, and delves beneath its surface to discover its verities and realities. A peace pilgrim seeks not a multiplicity of material things, but a simplification of material well-being, with need level as the ultimate goal. A peace pilgrim purifies the bodily temple, the thoughts, the desires, the motives. A peace pilgrim relinquishes as quickly as possible self-will, the feeling of separateness, all attachments, all negative feelings.

Now traditionally a pilgrim walks on faith without any visible means of support. I walk until given shelter. I fast until given food. It must be given, I never ask. But it is given!

Everything is given to me and I pass it on. You must give if you want to receive. Let the center of your being be one of giving, giving, giving. You can't give too much, and you will discover you cannot give without receiving. This kind of living is not reserved for the saints, but is available for little people like you and me — if we reach out to give to everybody.

It is my mission as a pilgrim to act as a messenger expressing spiritual truths. It is a task which I accept joyfully, and I desire nothing in return, neither praise or glory, nor the glitter of silver and gold. I simply rejoice to be able to follow the whisperings of a Higher Will.

I have much to offer: I deal primarily with living God's laws. I extend to others the mystical approach to God, the kingdom of inner peace. It is free, there is no charge.

⚶

There was a time — when I attained inner peace — when I died, utterly died to myself. I have since renounced my previous identity. I can see no reason to dwell upon my past, it is dead and should not be resurrected. Don't inquire of me — ask about my message. It's not important to remember the messenger, just remember the message.

⚶

Who am I? It matters not that you know who I am; it is of little importance. This clay garment is one of a penniless pilgrim journeying in the name of peace. It is what you cannot see that is so very important. I am one who is propelled by the power of faith; I bathe in the light of eternal wisdom; I am sustained by the unending energy of the universe; this is who I really am!

⚶

I always have a feeling of awe and wonder at what God can do — using me as an instrument. I believe that anyone who is fully surrendered to God's will can be used gloriously — and will really know some things — and will probably be called self-righteous. You're called self-righteous if you are self-centered enough to think you know everything — but you may also be called self-righteous by the immature if you are God-centered enough to really know some things.

⚶

My desire is to strive toward perfection; to be as much in harmony with God's will as possible; to live up to the highest light I have. I'm still not perfect, of course, but I grow daily. If I were perfect I would know everything and be able to do everything; I would be like God. However, I am able to do everything I am *called* to do, and I do know what I need to know to do my part in the

Divine Plan. And I do experience the happiness of living in harmony with God's will for me.

ℐ

Any praise I receive does not change me, for I pass it right along to God. I walk because God gives me the strength to walk, I live because God gives me the supply to live, I speak because God gives me the words to speak. All I did was to surrender my will to God's will. My entire life has prepared me for this undertaking. This is my calling. This is my vocation. This is what I must be doing. I could not be happy doing anything else.

ℐ

When I began my pilgrimage I left the Los Angeles area without a cent, having faith that God would provide me with everything I needed. Although I have never asked for anything, God has provided me with everything along the way. Without ever asking for anything I've been supplied.

I have faith that God will care for me, and God does provide my needs. I don't in any way feel insecure because I don't know where I will sleep at night, where or when I will eat next. When you have spiritual security, you have no more feeling of need for material security. I don't know anybody who feels more secure than I do — and, of course, people think I am the poorest of the poor. I know better, I am the richest of the rich. I have health, happiness, inner peace — things you couldn't buy if you were a billionaire.

ℐ

I do my work easily and joyously. I feel beauty all around me and I see beauty in everyone I meet, for I see God in everything. I recognize my part in the Life Pattern and I find harmony through gladly and joyously living it. I recognize my oneness with all mankind and my oneness with God. My happiness overflows in loving and giving toward everyone and everything.

For light I go directly to the Source of light, not to any of the reflections. Also I make it possible for more light to come to me by living up to the highest light I have. *You cannot mistake light coming from the Source, for it comes with complete understanding so that you can explain it and discuss it.* I recommend that way to all who can take it. And great blessings lie in store for those who are wise enough to quickly put into practice the highest light that comes to them.

ℐ

That which is received from without can be compared with knowledge. It leads to believing, which is seldom strong enough to motivate to action. That which is confirmed from within after it is contacted from without, or that which is directly perceived from within (which is my way) can be compared with wisdom. It leads to a knowing, and action goes right along with it.

ℐ

In my dealings with people, I don't chastise, nor do I issue edicts or lay down a blueprint. My appointed work is to awaken the divine nature that is within. This is my calling, to open doors of truth and make people think, to arouse others from their apathetic and lethargic state, and get them to seek out for themselves the inner peace which dwells within. This is the extent of my undertaking, I can do no more. The rest I leave to a higher power.

ℐ

Faith is a belief in things that your senses have not experienced and your mind does not understand, but you have touched them in other ways and have accepted them. It is easy for one to speak of faith; it is another thing to live it. To me, *faith* represents that people can, through their own free will, reach out and contact God, and *grace* represents that God is always reaching toward people. To me it is very important that I remain in constant contact with God, or divine purpose.

People have had to make up for their spiritual impoverishment by accumulating material things. When spiritual blessings come, material things seem unimportant. But spiritual blessings do not come until we desire them and relinquish desire for material things. As long as we desire material things this is all we receive, and we remain spiritually impoverished.

ℐ

Those who have overcome self-will and become instruments to do God's work can accomplish tasks which are seemingly impossible, but they experience no feeling of self achievement. I now know myself to be a part of the infinite cosmos, not separate from other souls or God. My illusory self is dead; the real self controls the garment of clay and uses it for God's work.

ℐ

When I started out, my hair had started to turn to silver. My friends thought I was crazy. There was not one word of encouragement from them. They thought I would surely kill myself, walking all over. But that didn't bother me. I just went ahead and did what I had to do. They didn't know that with inner peace I felt plugged into the source of universal energy, which never runs out. There was much pressure to compromise my beliefs, but I would not be dissuaded. Lovingly, I informed my well-meaning friends of the existence of two widely divergent paths in life and of the free will within all to make their choice.

There is a well-worn road which is pleasing to the senses and gratifies worldly desires, but leads to nowhere. And there is the less traveled path, which requires purifications and relinquishments, but results in untold spiritual blessings.

𝄢

There is a spark of good in everybody, no matter how deeply it may be buried. *It is the real you.* When I say 'you' what am I really thinking of? Am I thinking of the clay garment, the body? No, that's not the real you. Am I thinking of the self-centered nature? No, that's not the real you. The real you is that divine spark. Some call this the God-centered nature, others the divine nature and the Kingdom of God within. Hindus know it as nirvana; the Buddhists refer to it as the awakened soul; the Quakers see it as the Inner Light. In other places it is known as the Christ in you, the Christ Consciousness, the hope of glory, or the indwelling spirit. Even some psychologists have a name for it, the superconscious. But it is all the same thing dressed in different words. The important thing to remember is that it dwells within you!

𝄢

It does not matter what name you attach to it, but your consciouness must ascend to the point through which you view the universe with your God-centered nature. The feeling accompanying this experience is that of complete oneness with the Universal Whole. One merges into a euphoria of absolute unity with all life: with humanity, with all the creatures of the earth, the trees and plants, the air, the water, and even earth itself. This God-centered nature is constantly awaiting to govern your life gloriously. You have the free will to either allow it to govern your life, or not to allow it to affect you. This choice is always yours!

From all things you read, and from all people you meet, take what is good and leave the rest. For guidance and for truth it is much better to look for the Source through your own inner teacher than to look to people or books. Only if something within you says, *"This is the truth. This is for me,"* does it become a part of your experience. After you have read all the books, and heard all the lectures, you must still judge what is for you. Books and people can merely inspire you. Unless they awaken something within you, nothing worthwhile has been accomplished. But if you must read books, read many books, so that you will contact as many conflicting opinions as possible. In this manner you'll be required to form your own opinions after all.

Think about all the good things of your life. Never think about your difficulties. Forget yourself, and concentrate on being of service as much as you can in this world, and then, having lost your lower self in a cause greater than yourself, you will find your higher self: your real self.

What I speak of is not an easy undertaking, but I can assure you that the end of your spiritual journey will be well worth the price paid. There are many hills and valleys. The struggle is like climbing, with each hilltop a little higher than the last.

ᴔ

Some have asked if I accept 'disciples.' Of course, I do not. It is not healthy to follow another human being. Every person must find his or her maturity. The process takes time, the growth period is different for each individual.

Why do you look at me? Look at your own self. Why do you listen to me? Listen to your own self. Why do you believe in what I say? Do not believe in me or any other teacher, rather trust in your own inner voice. *This* is your guide, this is your teacher. Your teacher is within not without. Know yourself, not me!

Walk with me, but don't follow me blindly. Hold fast to the truth, not to my garments. My body is merely a clay structure; today it is here, tomorrow it shall be gone. If you attach yourself to me today, what are you going to do tomorrow when I am not with you? Attach yourself to God, attach yourself to humanity, only then will you be closer to me.

ᴔ

The path of the seeker is full of pitfalls and temptations, and the seeker must walk it alone with God. I would recommend that you keep your feet on the ground and your thoughts at lofty heights, so that you may attract only good. Concentrate on giving so that you may open yourself to receiving; concentrate on living according to the light you have so that you may open yourself to more light; get as much light as possible through the inner way. If such receiving seems difficult, look for some inspiration from a beautiful flower or a beautiful landscape, from some beautiful music or some beautiful words. However, that which is contacted from without must be confirmed within before it is yours.

𝒥

Remember that one who does an unworthy deed is in reality psychologically sick, and should be regarded with as much compassion as one who is physically sick. Remember that no one can hurt you except yourself. If someone does a mean thing to you, that person is hurt. You are not really hurt unless you become embittered, or unless you become angry and perhaps do a mean thing in return.

𝒥

I consider myself a server working on the *cause* of difficulties: *our immaturity.* And yet only a small minority are willing to work with cause. For every person working on cause there are thousands working on symptoms. I bless those who are working on the outer level to remove symptoms, but primarily I continue to work on the inner level to remove cause.

It is because most people have not found their purpose and function that they experience painful disharmony within, and thus the body of humanity is headed for chaos. Most of us fall short much more by omission than by commission: *"While the world perishes we go our way: purposeless, passionless, day after day."*

𝒥

In my work I have chosen the positive approach. I never think of myself as protesting against something, but rather as *witnessing for* harmonious living. Those who witness *for*, present solutions. Those who witness *against*, usually do not — they dwell on what is wrong, resorting to judgment and criticism and sometimes even name-calling. Naturally, the negative approach has a detrimental effect on the person who uses it, while the positive approach has a good effect. When an evil is attacked, the evil mobilizes, although it may have been weak and unorganized before, and therefore the attack gives it validity and strength. When there is no attack, but instead good influences are brought to bear upon the situation, not only does the evil tend to fade away, but the evildoer tends to be transformed. The positive approach inspires; the negative approach makes angry. When you make people angry, they act in accordance with their baser instincts, often violently and irrationally. When you inspire people, they act in accordance with their higher instincts, sensibly and rationally. Also, anger is transient, whereas inspiration sometimes has a life-long effect.

There is a criterion by which you can judge whether the thoughts you are thinking and the things you are doing are right for you. The criterion is: *Have they brought you inner peace?* If they have not, there is something wrong with them — so keep seeking! If what you do has brought you inner peace, stay with what you believe is right.

When you find peace within yourself, you become the kind of person who can live at peace with others. Inner peace is not found by staying on the surface of life, or by attempting to escape from life through any means. Inner peace is found by facing life squarely, solving its problems, and delving as far beneath its surface as possible to discover its verities and realities. Inner peace comes through strict adherence to the already quite well known laws of human conduct, such as the law that the means shape the end: that only a good means can ever attain a good end. Inner peace comes through relinquishment of self-will, attachments, and negative thoughts and feelings. Inner peace comes through working for the good of all. We are all cells in the body of humanity — all of us, all over the world. Each one has a contribution to make, and will know from within what this contribution is, but no one can find inner peace except by working, not in a self-centered way, but for the whole human family.

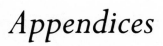

Appendices

Appendices

Capsule Summary of Peace Pilgrim's Life

190?: Born in eastern United States.

1938: Preparations begin. "Living to give instead of to get."

1953: January 1: Takes Peace Pilgrim as her name. Begins first cross-country pilgrimage from Pasadena, Calif.
December 17: Completes first pilgrimage at United Nations Building, New York City.

1954: Forty-five day fast.

1955: Begins second pilgrimage from San Francisco, Calif. Walks at least 100 miles in each state, visiting each of the state capitals. Also walks in Mexico and Canada.

1957: Walks 1000 miles in Canada — 100 miles in each of the Canadian provinces.

1964: Completes 25,000 miles on foot for peace at Washington, D.C. Stops counting miles, but continues to walk cross-country pilgrimage routes.

1966: Begins fourth pilgrimage.

1969: Begins fifth pilgrimage.

1973: Begins sixth pilgrimage.

1976: Visits Alaska and Hawaii for the first time.

1978: Begins seventh pilgrimage.

1979: June: Alaska educational and inspirational tour.

1980: August: Hawaii educational and inspirational tour.

1981: July 7: Passes to "a freer life" near Knox, Indiana, while on her seventh cross-country walk.

Peace Pilgrim's Chart of Her Spiritual Growth

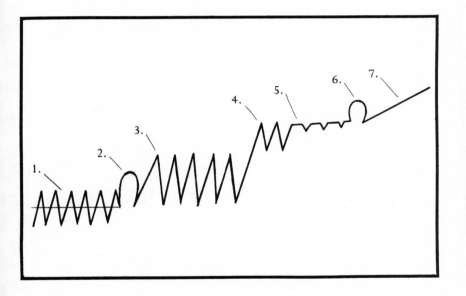

1. The ups and downs of emotion within the self-centered nature.
2. The first hump of no return: Complete willingness, without reservation, to give life to serve the higher will.
3. Battle between the God-centered nature and the self-centered nature.
4. First peak experience: A glimpse of inner peace.
5. Longer and longer plateaus of inner peace.
6. Complete inner peace.
7. Continuation of growth on a steadily upward path.

Questions and Answers from Correspondence

Peace Pilgrim considered it part of her job to reply to all of the thousands of people who wrote to her over the years. She picked up her mail at post offices all over the country — after it had been forwarded by her friend in Cologne, N.J. Concisely but thoughtfully she answered questions, commented on events, and told about her recent travels and travel plans. Her letters almost always began: "Greetings from South Dakota! (or Iowa or New Orleans . . .)"

Q: *How can I feel close to God?*

A: God is love, and whenever you reach out in loving kindness you are expressing God. God is truth, and whenever you seek truth you are seeking God. God is beauty, and whenever you touch the beauty of a flower or a sunset you are touching God. God is the intelligence that creates all and sustains all and binds all together and gives life to all. Yes, God is the essence of all — so you are within God and God is within you — you could not be where God is not. Permeating all is the law of God — physical law and spiritual law. Disobey it and you feel unhappiness: you feel separated from God. Obey it and you feel harmony: you feel close to God. As you live in harmony with divine law you will feel closer to and develop more love for God.

Q: *What is the very heart of successful human relations?*

A: Loving people, seeing the good in them, knowing that each one is important and has his or her job to do in the divine plan.

Q: *Can spiritual growth be accomplished quickly or does it take awhile?*

A: Spiritual growth is a process the same as physical growth or mental growth. Five year old children do not expect to be as tall as their parents at their next birthday; the first grader does not expect to graduate into college at the end of the term; the truth student should not expect to attain inner peace overnight. It took me fifteen years. The spiritual growing up is a very interesting and enjoyable process. There should be no wish to either hasten it or slow it down. Just experience it and take the steps toward inner peace and let it unfold.

Q: *How can one find inner peace?*

A: To find inner peace, or happiness, you must go through the spiritual growing up, you must leave the self-centered life and enter the God-centered life — the life in which you see yourself as part of the whole and work for the good of the whole.

Q: *You have said that perfect love is the key to happiness. Buddha seemed to say it was a matter of controlling the mind — "To enjoy good health, to bring true happiness to one's family, to bring peace to all, one must first discipline and control one's own mind. If a man can control his mind he can find the way to enlightenment, and all wisdom and virtue will naturally come to him."*

A: Perfect love is a willingness to give without a thought of receiving anything in return. When you have achieved that spiritual state, you will be in complete control of your mind — as well as your body and your emotions.

Q: *You have said that you have a calling. Do all human beings have a calling?*

A: Yes, all human beings have a calling, which is revealed to them through an awakening of their God-centered nature.

Q: *Are we here to serve humanity as well as learn our lessons?*

A: Yes, and we must serve according to our calling. We must also learn to live in harmony with divine law — but that is part of learning our lessons. As you live harmoniously and outgoingly you grow spiritually.

Q: *What is the goal and purpose of mankind?*

A: Our goal and purpose is to bring our lives into harmony with God's will.

Q: *What is God?*

A: We lump together all things that are beyond the capacity of all of us collectively to understand — and one name we give to all those things together is God. Therefore, God is the creative force, the sustaining power, that which motivates toward constant change, the overall intelligence which governs the universe by physical and spiritual law, truth, love, goodness, kindness, beauty, the ever-present, all-pervading essence or spirit, which binds everything in the universe together and gives life to everything in the universe.

Q: *Why are people unhappy?*

A: People are unhappy because they are out of harmony with God's will.

Q: *Do problems have their foundation in a poor self-concept?*
A: Problems come when we live our lives out of harmony with divine purpose — they come to push us toward harmony.

Q: *In your opinion, what is the number one world problem?*
A: The number one world problem is immaturity. We choose to live at a small fraction of our real potential. In our immaturity we are greedy: some grab more than their share so that others starve. In our immaturity we are fearful: we build up armaments against one another, resulting in war. If we work on world problems, we usually work at the level of symptom. I have chosen to work primarily at the level of removing cause.

Q: *Is the goal of self-knowledge to know God?*
A: If you really know yourself you will know you are a child of God and you will become aware of God.

Q: *What is mysticism?*
A: One who takes the mystic approach receives direct perceptions from within. This is the source from which all truth came in the first place.

Q: *How can one get the answers from within, from one's soul?*
A: When you say "soul" you mean the divine nature, whereas some would mean the self-centered nature and some would mean both. Your divine nature — a drop of God — can be awakened when you touch a truth from outside, so that it confirms that truth. Or the truth can come directly from the inside. Have an inspirational time and fill your life with inspirational things to awaken your divine nature.

Q: *Where did you learn meditation?*
A: I did not learn meditation. I just walked, receptive and silent, amid the beauty of nature — and put the wonderful insights that came to me into practice.

Q: *Do you suggest to the seeker meditation or breathing exercises?*
A: I suggest a time apart or a time alone with God, walking in receptive silence amid the beauties of God's nature. From the beauty of nature you get your inspiration, from the silent receptiveness you get your meditation, from the walking you get not only exercise but breathing — all in one lovely experience.

Q: *Can one's divine nature be awakened through meditation?*
A: If you are really meditating, your body is so comfortable that you are not aware of it. Your emotions are serenely still. Your mind is at peace — waiting, but not pushing. Now that you are receptive and silent,

divine receiving can take place through your divine nature. *It is very important that you put into practice insights that come to you.*

Q: *What is the kundalini?*

A: The awakening of the kundalini could originally have meant the awakening of the divine nature — but some I know use the word to mean plugging into the source of universal energy.

Q: *What does it mean to awaken the kundalini?*

A: Those who are interested in forcing spiritual growth think about awakening the kundalini. Those who have good sense live in a spiritual life and await spiritual unfoldment.

Q: *Can you describe intuition?*

A: Real intuition is a spiritual receiving through the divine nature — but I realize that psychic receiving is sometimes referred to as intuition.

Q: *Do you love humanity or people?*

A: We are all of equal worth in the eyes of God, and to all I reach out constantly in thoughts and words and deeds — with love and good wishes — with prayers and blessings. This it is to love humanity. However, people are the cells in the body of humanity, and in doing my part in the divine plan I come into contact with a few of these cells. When their lives touch mine, I am always willing and sometimes able to serve them. When I am with someone or in correspondence with someone, I concentrate my love and my good wishes on that particular cell I am touching, and then with my prayers and blessings I leave that cell in God's hands. This it is to love people. Some love humanity without loving people; some love people without loving humanity. I love both.

Q: *What is good and what is evil?*

A: At a simple level, good is that which helps people; evil is that which hurts people. At a higher level, good is that which is in harmony with divine purpose; evil is that which is out of harmony with divine purpose.

Q: *Often I tell myself that good is stronger than evil, love stronger than hatred, that good must win, but will it win in this world?*

A: Yes, good will win in this world. The darkness that we see in the world today is due to the disintegration of things which are not good. Only the things which are good can endure. Yes, love will win in this world. Those who are filled with hatred are desperately unhappy and desperately — even though unconsciously — seeking a better way. Only those who are filled with love are serene and at peace.

Q: *How can one break bad habits of thought and action?*

A: Bad habits of thought and action lessen as spiritual growth progresses. You can work on replacing negative thoughts with positive thoughts. If it is a negative thought about a person, dwell upon *a good thing* about that person. If it is a negative thought about a world situation, dwell upon the *best* that could happen in that situation. You can deliberately refrain from a bad action — and use the energy for a good action.

Q: *Are you willing to forgive people who do evil things even before they are sorry?*

A: I do not even need to forgive people, for I harbor no animosity. If they do evil things I feel compassion for them because I know they have hurt themselves. I hope they will be sorry, because I want them to be healed.

Q: *Do you have any thoughts on improving the health profession?*

A: Needful and gradually coming into manifestation are health centers which will stress coming into and remaining in good health by coming into and remaining in harmony with the physical and spiritual laws. This is the healing of the future. I think there has been too much tendency to just let people get sick, and then look for ways to help them. I believe the emphasis should be on keeping people well, therefore I think in terms of health research. We have been alleviating symptoms too long — let us get busy on eliminating cause.

Q: *Is the goal of the spiritual nature to free itself from the body or physical nature in order that it may see truth clearly?*

A: The spiritual nature does see truth clearly. If you let it govern your life, you will see truth clearly. You might say that the spiritual nature is trying to free you from the self-centered nature, so you will become an entity living in harmony with divine purpose.

Q: *If we can go on the presumption that everyone has a spiritual nature, why do so few people realize it? Are they being punished for misdeeds in a past life, or are they just unenlightened in this life?*

A: Because they have free will. They punish themselves by making wrong choices. Constantly enlightenment is being offered to them, but they refuse to accept it. Therefore, they are being taught by problems that are set before them, since they refuse to make right choices voluntarily.

Q: *Why can this world be so confusing?*

A: People disobey divine law, so problems come to push them toward harmony. If you but knew how short is the earth life in comparison with the whole, you would be less troubled with the difficulties of the earth life than you are troubled now with the difficulties of one of your days.

Q: *When does illumination come?*

A: The time when you rise high enough in consciousness to look at things through the eyes of the God-centered nature is often called the illumination experience.

Q: *Does God speak through you?*

A: In a sense, God speaks through everyone whose life is governed by God.

Q: *Did you experience a divine revelation? If so, why were you chosen as a person God could reveal his spiritual knowledge to?*

A: I had a very strong inner motivation, or calling, to begin my pilgrimage, and I started out against the advice of all my friends. I chose myself to be a receiver of spiritual truth when I surrendered my will to God's will. You can do that too. We all have the same potential. God is revealed to all who seek, *God speaks to all who will listen.* When you surrender your will to God's will you enter a very busy life — and a very beautiful life.

Q: *Is the self-centered nature an illusion?*

A: The self-centered nature is transient, just as the body is transient — but it is up to us how soon it will cease to rule our lives.

Q: *Is there a law of self-responsibility?*

A: You are responsible for your actions, reactions or inaction where action is required. You owe right living not only to humanity, but to yourself.

Q: *What is your Utopia like? Can there ever be a Utopia in this earth life?*

A: The outer Utopia would come when we have learned to share and not to kill each other. The inner Utopia would come when we have all found inner peace. A lot of us will have to find a lot more inner peace before the outer Utopia can come. The outer is forseeable — the inner will take a lot longer.

Q: *Is there a God who will always be beyond me?*

A: Think of God as a divine ocean and you as one drop with free will. You can choose to remain separate from the ocean — but you won't be happy. You can choose to be a part of the ocean, in which case you will give up your free will, but you will be delightfully happy acting in harmony with God's will. Now you will perceive yourself as a part of God and very much at one with God.

Q: *What is the spiritual life?*

A: That which cannot be perceived by the five senses. Spiritual things will endure, physical things will not.

Q: *What is truth?*

A: Truth is that which is in harmony with divine law. Truth is God and God is truth. My personal prayer is to make me an instrument through which only truth can speak.

Q: *Where do I look to find spiritual truth?*

A: In the final analysis you find spiritual truth through your own higher nature. Your higher nature is a drop in the ocean of God — and has access to the ocean. Sometimes your higher nature is awakened through the inspiration of beautiful surroundings or beautiful music, bringing you insights of truth. Sometimes you see the truth written or hear the truth spoken, and your higher nature confirms it. Or you directly perceive the truth from the inside through an awakening of the higher nature, which is my way. All the inspired writing came from the inner source, and you too, can receive from that source. Be still and know.

Q: *Will there always be pain in one's becoming more beautiful?*

A: There will be pain in your spiritual growth until you will to do God's will and no longer need to be pushed into it. When you are out of harmony with God's will, problems come. Their purpose is to push you into harmony. If you would willingly do God's will, you could avoid the problems.

Q: *Will I ever come to a state of feeling at rest with no more need to become?*

A: When you have found inner peace you have no more feeling of need to become — you are content to be, which includes following your divine guidance. However, you keep on growing — but harmoniously.

Q: *I am so lonely. What can I do about it?*

A: You are never really alone. God is always with you. Turn to God for the best possible companionship. Turn to books and music for inspiration. Turn to the phone to say words of cheer to a shut-in, or visit one who is lonely. In giving we receive, and our loneliness fades away.

Q: *How do you keep so healthy and happy?*

A: I keep so healthy and happy by always keeping turned to God. That means I obey God's spiritual laws: I live to be of service, I think no negative thoughts, etc. That means I obey God's physical laws: those things I know are bad for the health I do not do, those things I know are good for the health I do. My reward has been good health and a happy state of mind.

Q: *How does an ordinary housewife and mother find what you seem to possess?*

A: One who is in the family pattern, as most people are, finds inner peace in the same way that I found it. Obey God's laws, which are the same for all of us; not only the physical laws, but also the spiritual laws which govern human conduct. You might start by living all the good things you believe, as I did. Find and fit into your special place in the divine plan, which is unique for every human soul. You might try seeking in receptive silence, as I did. Being in the family pattern is not a block to spiritual growth, and in some ways it is an advantage. We grow through problem-solving, and being in the family pattern provides plenty of problems to grow on. When people enter the family pattern they often have their first outgoingness from self-centeredness into family-centeredness. Pure love is a willingness to give without a thought of receiving anything in return, and the family pattern provides the first experience of pure love: a mother's and father's love for their baby.

Q: *Why are you a vegetarian, and how can you be sure you are consistent?*

A: As to my vegetarianism, I do the best I can. I have never refrained from doing something I believed was right because I could not do it perfectly. I do not believe it is right for me to ask someone else to do my 'dirty work' for me. I would not kill a creature, and I would not ask someone else to kill it for me, so I will not eat the flesh of the creature.

Q: *My husband must go into surgery, but he is postponing it. What shall I do?*

A: If your husband must go into surgery, it is important that he go into it with as little apprehension as possible. A lady I knew faced a similar problem. She discussed it with her husband, and was able to convince him that God requires us to do everything we can for ourselves. So they undertook eating habits and living habits that they thought would be best for them. They planned to go to a beautiful and quiet place for the recuperation period, and they planned for a lovely trip afterward. He became impatient to get surgery over with so he would feel good enough to enjoy the things they had planned. It turned out to be minor instead of major, the recuperation period seemed like a vacation, and the trip seemed like a second honeymoon.

Q: *I, along with all the other non-smokers, was thankful when you asked people not to smoke at your meeting, but I was wondering if you were being loving toward the smokers.*

A: A pilgrim's job of rousing people from their apathy and making them think may sometimes seem to come into conflict with a loving attitude toward people. However, if I saw a small child about to touch a red hot stove, I would certainly prevent the child from doing so if I could — and this would be a loving thing for me to do, although the child might not like it and might even scream. A woman wrote recently to tell me that when I refused to sit next to her because she was smoking she stayed awake for hours thinking about it — and cut out smoking the next day.

Q: *My husband is a cigarette smoker and I cannot stand the smoke. Could you tell me what to do?*

A: Evidently you are allergic to tobacco smoke, and therefore you should never be in a room where someone is smoking. Some smoke, like wood smoke, is not poisonous. But tobacco smoke is poisonous, and certainly not good for anyone. Of course it would be good for him and for you if your husband would stop smoking, but if he doesn't want to do that, he should never smoke in a room where you are. Could he smoke outdoors or in some part of the house reserved for him or in some place away from home? No use quarreling about this. It's best to use your energy to find a solution.

Q: *How does one transform a desire such as smoking or drinking instead of suppressing it?*

A: When it comes to such things as smoking and drinking I would just quit, as I quit the caffeine habit long ago by making a quick relinquishment. However, some prefer to substitute. I just met a lady who is substituting tea brewed from mint leaves for coffee. I know another lady who has substituted fruit juice for cocktails, and she says her friends don't even know it yet. A man I know has put a little package of raisins and nuts into the pocket where he once kept cigarettes. It can be done.

Q: *Should we reach outward or upward?*

A: We should always be reaching upward for light — while reaching outward in love to those who need our help. Yes, as one walks the spiritual pathway, one looks up for guidance and reaches out in giving. Therefore, associates are not only those more evolved from whom we learn, but also those less evolved who come for help.

Q: *Why does God exist?*

A: God is the life force without which the universe would not exist. God is expressed throughout the physical and spiritual universe.

Q: *What is one's relationship to God?*

A: You can establish a relationship with God by bringing your life into harmony with God's laws, which are the same for all of us. And by finding and fitting into your part in the divine plan, which is unique for every human soul.

Q: *Who is Jesus?*

A: Jesus was a great spiritual teacher who walked the earth. His life was governed by the indwelling Christ. He taught us ours could be too.

Q: *What do you tell people who ask if you are a Christian?*

A: I am not, and have never been, a part of any particular faith. I am a deeply religious woman who has taken the inner way to a religious life, not the scholarly way or the way of early training. I will never say this is the only way. It is, of course, an excellent way. And people are free to choose and develop in their own way.

Q: *Do you believe that Jesus Christ is the savior of mankind or do you believe that he was not different from anyone else but was only more spiritually evolved?*

A: Jesus was a very evolved being, way ahead of his time. Christ is the divine nature, which can rule your life as it ruled his life. The indwelling Christ is the 'savior of mankind.' Only when it governs your life will you be happy.

Q: *Do you believe in the second coming of Jesus Christ?*

A: All who believe in the continuity of life (and some who do not) believe that Jesus could return. I believe we should allow the indwelling Christ or the divine nature to govern our lives.

Q: *What did Jesus mean by teaching of a kingdom "not of this world?"*

A: He was teaching about the Kingdom of God within, the God-centered nature, the divine nature — the indwelling Christ.

Q: *What is the first priority of life?*

A: Jesus said, "Seek ye first the kingdom of God and his righteousness. All these things shall be added unto you." This is true. All the blessings are beyond anything that I could possibly describe in words. Health, happiness, inner peace, and always with you an awareness of the presence of God. A complete stability of unhurriedness. Fear is absolutely gone from your life. You cannot feel fear because when you know that God is right there, naturally you're with God.

Q: *If you have grown up spiritually, how come you are not famous?*

A: Most people who have attained inner peace are not famous.

Q: *Are you an Avatar, a divine incarnation?*

A: I am a pilgrim for peace, inner peace and outer peace. I walk in prayer for peace. I try to inspire others to pray and work for peace also. I would gladly be a 'server': one who returns again and again to help people toward a more spiritual life.

Q: *Is the Messiah concept immature? Was Jesus the Messiah? Are you a Messiah?*

A: Yes, the Messiah concept is immature. Immature people look for a Messiah instead of looking for the Christ within. Jesus was a great spiritual teacher. I am teaching how to live God's laws. In each being there is a divine nature called by various names. After sufficient lifetimes it begins to govern the being. That being stands out from the crowd. There have been quite a few. The important thing is that it can govern you.

Q: *Why did man invent dogma?*

A: Dogma was not necessarily invented; it springs from ignorance and fear and immaturity. It is sometimes used against immature people by the unscrupulous. People believe in dogma because they are trained to believe in it.

Q: *Why do people believe in dogmatic religion?*

A: Immature people believe in immature religion because they are afraid not to. As they mature enough to know it is immature they tend to depart from it.

Q: *Would you describe dogma?*

A: Take out the kernel of spiritual truth within any faith, and what is left is dogma.

Q: *What is it like to communicate with God?*

A: Communication with God is a deep inner knowing that God is within you and around you. God 'speaks' through the still, small voice within.

Q: *Are science and religion irreconcilable?*

A: You might say that science operates pragmatically and religion by divine guidance. If valid, they would reach the same conclusions but science would take a lot longer.

Q: *Would you describe spritual evolution?*

A: Spiritual evolution takes place in your life as you live in harmony with divine purpose: obeying divine laws, which are the same for all of us, and doing your unique job in the divine plan.

Q: *Atheists say there is no way to prove that there is a God. Can you prove that there is a God?*

A: There is really no such thing as an atheist, for within that person is the divine nature which, when awakened, will feel close to God. There are those who call themselves atheists. For some of them I have defined

God *intellectually* as the creative force, the sustaining power, the motivation toward change, the overall intelligence, truth; *emotionally* as love, goodness, kindness, beauty; *spiritually* as the ever-present, all-pervading essence or spirit, which binds everything in the universe together and gives life to everything in the universe.

Q: *Can the creation of the universe be some grandiose accident?*

A: The universe is the creation of an intelligence which we cannot now even imagine — and we have the wonderful opportunity of learning and growing in it.

Q: *What is the nature of the universe?*

A: The nature of the universe is an evolvement toward betterment or perfection.

Q: *When was the physical universe created and when will it be destroyed?*

A: We do not know the exact time of the beginning of the universe, although we try to figure it out. Of course, we don't know the time of the end either, and we do less speculating on that. All we can really say is: it began when it was necessary in creation, it will end when it is no longer necessary. It is very much needed now, and one of the lessons we must learn is to live in the present, instead of trying to live in the past or the future. Of course, one of the lessons we must learn is that we are really spiritual, in fact, that is our most important lesson. You can say it is our goal, and the goal of evolution. However, our immediate goal is to bring our lives into harmony with divine law and do the work we came to do.

Q: *Do you believe that there is both a heaven and a hell?*

A: Heaven and hell are states of being. Heaven is being in harmony with God's will; hell is being out of harmony with God's will. You can be in either state on either side of life. There is no permanent hell.

Q: *Do we have experiences before the earth life and after the earth life?*

A: There is a point of view which recognizes the experience of the earth life as you recognize the experience of one of your days — with days coming before and days lying ahead. Just as you know that what you did yesterday can affect tomorrow, so the viewpoint I speak of recognizes that prior experience affects this earth life and that this earth life will affect future experience. To those with this viewpoint the world is orderly and just and operates according to law. When the governing laws are obeyed there is harmony and when they are disobeyed there is discord. This cannot be seen by those whose horizons do not extend beyond the earth life. To them the world must seem very unjust and very disorderly indeed.

Q: *Why do people fear death?*

A: Almost all fear is fear of the unknown. People fear death because what happens at death is unknown. However, I have experienced the beginning of the process called death — in a snowstorm one night when I began to freeze to death — and I do not fear it. The experience of the beginning of the change called death I went through that night was beautiful. I look forward to the change called death as life's last great adventure, and I rejoice with my loved ones as they make the glorious transition to a freer living. You overcome your fear of something by becoming acquainted with the thing you fear.

Q: *If one fears death, does that mean one has a poor self-concept?*

A: Fear of death tends to mean that you identify with the body instead of the spirit, and that is poor self-concept.

Q: *Do you think a soul can leave the body before the preordained time?*

A: It is true that this universe operates according to exact laws. It is true that some come into an earth life only to stay for a very short time. Some come in only to stay until certain things are accomplished. Some come in to stay as long as the body will last. You can come in to learn lessons, to pay debts, to serve, or a combination of these things. Through it all, you have free will. If you take good care of your body, you stay longer than if you abuse it. Thoughts and emotions also play a part. So you see things are really only conditionally preordained — you will stay a long time *if*.

Q: *If the spiritual nature is immortal, what does it do after the death of the body? Is the spiritual nature always good in each body?*

A: If the self-centered nature has been completely overcome, the spiritual nature — the real you — will go to the spiritual realm instead of the psychic realm. It will now no longer need to live more earth lives, and will be learning other lessons. The spiritual nature is always good and always consistent with God's will. It is the self-centered nature that is sometimes passive, sometimes good, sometimes out of harmony.

Q: *What is karma?*

A: Karma is the law of cause and effect — *'as you sow so shall you reap'* — seen over a span of many lifetimes. Those who get ulcers as a result of hating someone prove to themselves (if they have the eyes to see) that the law of karma works.

Q: *Some problems seem inherited or chronic. Are these things karmic?*

A: Every problem that comes to you has a purpose in your life. Through problem solving you learn and grow. No problem is set before you that, with a proper attitude, you cannot solve. If a great problem is set before you, this indicates that you have the great inner strength to solve a great problem. Some problems that are brought over with you are karmic — subject to the law of cause and effect. You might say you came to solve them. It is important that they be solved. That's at least one of the reasons you came. Some problems are caused in this earth life by wrong eating, or wrong thinking and feeling. They might be caused by eating junk food, or thinking junk thoughts, like hate thoughts. While tendencies toward certain difficulties can be inherited, remember you choose the conditions of your birth. I wish for all a complete healing — not through the suppression of symptoms by drugs, but through the removal of cause. I hope you will be inspired to put yourself on a really excellent health diet. I hope you will be inspired to search for and remove all negative thoughts and feelings. I hope you will be inspired to fill your life with beautiful things — the beauty of nature, uplifting music, beautiful words and meaningful activities. Stay away from everything that pulls you down, and stick to the things that lift you up!

Q: *What is the best way to 'pay off' bad karma?*
A: The best way to rid yourself of all bad karma is to get busy serving in any way you can. When you have given enough, you will know God and find inner peace — for it is in giving that we receive.

Q: *Can I experience past life recall?*
A: You may very well recall some past life experiences when you have learned the lessons you came here to learn. Before that it is best not to know such things — you would be less likely to solve the problem if you already had the answer. There is an old hymn that says, "I do not ask to see the distant scene, one step enough for me." That is very wise.

Q: *Can my divine nature control my anger and rage?*
A: Your divine nature can control your body, your mind and your emotions. Your self-centered nature cannot, although it can rule them to a certain extent. Anger-energy should not be suppressed, which could hurt you inside, nor expressed, which would hurt you inside and cause difficulties in your surroundings. It should be *transformed* by using it for a task that needs to be done or a beneficial form of exercise. If you will realize that the person who does an unkind thing is to some extent psychologically sick, anger will turn to compassion.

Q: *How can people improve their self-confidence?*
A: Your self-confidence will improve when you realize who you are. You are God's child, and capable of acting that way.

Q: *In this affluent country why do so many complain about financial problems?*

A: Many people who say they have financial problems really mean that they want more than they need. It was so easy for me to bring my life down to need level: I just felt that I could no longer accept more than I need while others in the world have less than they need. I discover in looking around me that most debts are not to pay for the necessities of life, but to pay for things people do not need. Why do people want things they do not need? Sometimes for purposes of self-indulgence — when they will never find what they are seeking except through self-discipline. Sometimes to gain ego-satisfaction by impressing others — when they will never find what they are seeking until the ego has been subordinated and the higher nature has taken over. Yes, some do try to make up for a lack of spiritual security with material security — and it can't be done. Financial problems come to teach us that our concentration should not be on material things, but on spiritual things. I'm sure you know the wonderful purpose of problems in our lives, how they all come to teach us lessons, and how we can always solve them with God's help.

Q: *What should be our attitude toward material things?*

A: If we could just put material things into their proper place, and use them without being attached to them, how much freer we would be. Then we wouldn't burden ourselves with things we don't need. If we could only realize that we are all cells in the same body of humanity — then we would think of having enough for all, not too much for some and too little for others.

Q: *What about the predictions of destruction?*

A: Remember the power of thought, and think only about the best that could happen. Dwell only upon the good things you want to see happen. Remember, through thought you create your inner conditions and help to create the conditions around you. We are all helping to make a great decision. Remember also that the darkest hour is just before the dawn.

Q: *What can I do about my grandchild coming into the world that is filled with violence?*

A: Why not think of your grandchild as being born into a world filled with God? God's law is implemented constantly, for everything out of harmony is on its way out. The darkness we see is the disintegration of out-of-harmony things. *"God is not dead, nor doth he sleep . . . the wrong shall fail, the right prevail . . . with peace on earth, good will to men."* How can anyone doubt that eventually God will prevail? It is only how soon that is up to us.

Q: *What are your solutions to the following problems:*

The Energy Crisis?

A: There should be intensive research of all forms of clean energy — sun power, wind power, water power including wave power. In some places thermal energy is available. I stayed on a ranch which with solar panels and two windmills provided its own energy.

Terrorism?

A: Terrorists are extremely immature and also usually wrongly trained people who believe that evil can be overcome by more evil. They need a healing program to bring about their rehabilitation.

Organized Crime?

A: Organized crime is a symptom of an immature society in which success is measured by money and things. Those connected with it need a healing program for their rehabilitation.

Gangs and gang warfare?

A: Youth gangs could be prevented if there were plenty of room for children to play in good surroundings and meaningful organized activities for youth.

Absenteeism?

A: Much absenteeism comes about because people are doing jobs they do not feel called to do. People should take jobs they like best to do, rather than jobs that pay the most money.

Jealousy?

A: Immature people are jealous because they do not know they are just as important as anyone else, with just as much potential, and with a job in the divine plan.

Hatred and Racism?

A: You can overcome hatred with love. Hate injures the hater, not the hated. Those who practice racism are hurt. Those that are discriminated against have a choice: They can be hurt by a wrong reaction of bitterness or anger, or they can rise above the situation and be spiritually strengthened.

Frustration?

A: The self-centered nature feels frustration when it can't have its way. The higher nature is patient, knowing that with a proper attitude all problems can be solved.

Suffering?

A: It is an orderly universe, and the suffering that comes to us has a purpose in our lives — it is trying to teach us something. We should look for its lesson.

Q: *Are you a liberal or a conservative?*

A: I am conservative in wanting to preserve the good things — I am a liberal in wanting to change the things that need to be changed.

Q: *What is your political and social philosophy?*

A: Our politics and our social order must be brought into harmony with divine purpose.

Q: *What do you think of capitalism?*

A: If by capitalism you mean our present economic system which has led to unemployment and production for obsolescence, naturally this will need to be improved. More decentralization is needed. If those who worked in the industries also owned the industries, much friction could be avoided. Capitalism usually means competition — and the work for the future is cooperation.

Q: *Do you think democracy is the right form of government?*

A: If democracy is control by the people, as it is supposed to be, it is the right form of government. I believe in a complete democracy — individual, political, social, economic. If we really had that, which we don't now, it would be in harmony with divine purpose.

Q: *What are leftists and what are rightists?*

A: Those who want to push social change faster than it can naturally go are often called 'leftists'. Those who want to keep things as they are or turn back the hands of the clock are often called 'rightists'. In general they have one thing in common: they both believe in the false philosophy that 'the end justifies the means'. That is the war philosophy. I believe that the means you use will determine the end you receive. This is the peace philosophy and the philosophy of all true religion. Your divine nature lives by the peace philosophy.

Q: *Do you believe that communism could take over the world and wipe out religion?*

A: Of course religion will endure, since it represents the deep inner yearning for a better life of all human beings. Communism at its best represents communal living — sharing. As practiced in some small societies it is not an enemy of religion. It has never really been practiced in any large society, and the first large society to express it is an ideal turned against the religion of the state because they felt it had been used to oppress people. Then they became a dictatorship. The things that are out of harmony in their country and our country, and all countries, are in the process of disintegrating — they contain within themselves the seeds of their own destruction. True communism could teach the world something about economic democracy.

Q: *Do you think communists could end the world by starting a nuclear war?*

A: No, I don't think any country really wants to start a nuclear war. But it could happen by accident as long as we have all these nuclear weapons around.

Q: *Is it good to learn an art like karate in order to defend oneself?*

A: My weapon is love, and I would not even think of learning any other defense mechanism. The immature and the fearful learn karate and other defense mechanisms.

Q: *Does 'passive' mean peaceful to you? Does aggressive mean warlike to you?*

A: You could say that a passive person does not use violence because of weakness, and a *peaceful* person does not use violence because of principle. An aggressive person may prefer to live in harmony but the actions of that person lead to strife.

Q: *Men commit 88% of all crimes as well as fight in all the wars. Of course there are a few exceptions, but do you believe that in general women are more mature and law-abiding than men? Are they more spiritually evolved?*

A: Men are taught that they must be tough, and that it is a sign of weakness to live by the law of love. It is considered perfectly all right for women to live by the law of love; in fact, in many cases this is expected of them. Men have just as much spiritual potential as women, but because of their more aggressive attitudes they often do not attain as much spiritual growth. In our country the men fight the wars because that is the custom here, but in some countries the women fight too.

Q: *How should parents punish their children when they do something wrong?*

A: The reward system works best; punishment would be withholding the reward.

Q: *What is immorality?*

A: Sometimes when people talk about immorality they mean that which is out of harmony with custom. But true immorality is that which is out of harmony with divine purpose.

Q: *Is the mind a "blank tablet" on which experience writes?*

A: The mind is an instrument which can be used by either the self-centered nature or the divine nature. Yes, of course it is influenced by experience.

Q: *What is your interpretation of dreams?*

A: Most dreams represent either wanderings in the psychic realm or illusions produced by physical or mental or emotional stresses, and should be promptly forgotten. A few times there is a vision, which you will not be able to forget.

Q: *Do you work for your living?*

A: I work for my living in an unusual way. I give what I can through thoughts and words and deeds to those whose lives I touch and to humanity. In return I accept what people want to give, but I do not ask. They are blessed by their giving and I am blessed by my giving.

Q: *Why are you unemployed?*

A: Am I unemployed? I work 16 hours a day, seven days a week. You mean I'm not earning any money. I don't need to earn any money. Everything I need is given. I could do this another way at my season of life. I could legally live on the taxpayers (Social Security) if I wanted to, but they give so reluctantly. I would much rather live on what is given voluntarily. Those people will be blessed by the giving. I love my work. I have work to do. For the kind of speaking I do, some people receive high honorariums; I do not accept one. I answer lots of mail and do a lot of counseling through the mail. Many people are paid good fees for counseling. I don't accept money for it. I am now starting to lead educational and inspirational tours which are retreat situations. It has a good effect on people. I remember the time we went to Alaska. Those people who went came back inspired and uplifted and it seems that just about every one of them is thinking about working for some good cause or a kind of a path of service. I believe some of those people from the Alaska trip are actually working now to help people.

Q: *Why don't you accept money?*

A: Because I talk about spiritual truth, and spiritual truth should never be sold — those who sell it injure themselves spiritually. I accept money that comes in through the mail (without being solicited), but I do not use it for myself; I use it for printing and postage. Those who attempt to buy spiritual truth are attempting to get it before they are ready. In this wonderfully well-ordered universe, when they are ready it will be given.

Q: *What is the theory behind 'not buying spiritual truth'?*

A: The theory behind not buying spiritual truth is this: One who has it would not be selling it, so one who is selling it doesn't have it. These are the 'pearls without price'. As soon as you are ready for the spiritual truth, it will be given. On the other hand, you are given as you give. But paying a fee is not giving a gift. And you do not need to give to the one from whom you receive, as we are all cells in the same body of humanity.

Q: *Don't you get lonely or discouraged or tired?*

A: No, I am never lonely or discouraged or tired. When you live in constant communion with God, you cannot be lonely. When you perceive the working of God's wonderful plan and know that all good effort bears good fruit, you cannot be discouraged. When you have found inner peace, you are in contact with the source of universal energy and cannot be tired.

Q: *Where did you learn the things you talk about? Obviously you have found something which all of us are seeking, and you have no right to conceal the source of your information.*

A: I have never concealed the source of my information. For light I go directly to the Source of Light — not to any of the reflections. Also, I make it possible for more light to come to me by living up to the highest light I have. You cannot mistake light coming from the source, for it comes with complete understanding so that you can explain it and discuss it.

Q: *How old are you?*

A: Along my pilgrimage route many people would ask my age. I told them I did not know my age and I did not intend to figure it out. I know my birth date. It lingers at the fringes of my memory, but I won't divulge it. What purpose would it serve? Many have tried also to guess my old name. The most interesting guess was that I'm Amelia Earhart. I'm very thankful that age is now out of my mind. As long as I counted birthdays and started thinking about getting older, I did get older. Age is a state of mind, and I think of myself as ageless. And that's my advice to others. Get to be as old as you want to be and then stop creating age.

I never give out my zodiac sign either. Do you honestly think I can be pushed around by a planet? Good heavens, your divine nature is always free — it's only your self-centered nature that is not free. I have two reasons for not giving out my sign. One is that some enterprising astrologer might figure out a horoscope on me, and what a waste of time that would be. And if my birth time were known I would be deluged by birthday cards just as I am deluged with Christmas cards now, and I would have to take another two weeks off each year to answer them.

Q: *What is your real name and background?*

A: I have no name except Peace Pilgrim. I have no home, only a forwarding address: Cologne, New Jersey. About my background I will say only this: I come from a poor family, I have little education, no special talents; rather, I lead a guided life.

Q: *Have you ever had any children?*

A: I was not called into the family pattern. Most people are, by this thing we call falling in love, and then they act as a family unit. It was not my calling. There are a few people not called into the family pattern. Some unmarried women are what you would call man-haters, but I'm not or ever was. I always got along fine with men.

Q: *How do you have so much energy?*

A: After you have found inner peace you have endless energy — the more you give, the more you receive. After you have found your calling, you work easily and joyously. You never get tired.

Q: *Doesn't the generation gap keep you from relating to students?*

A: I think it is a *value* gap rather than a generation gap. Students are in rebellion against false values of society like war and prejudice and materialism and hypocrisy. Since I certainly do not favor these false values, I have no trouble relating to students.

Q: *Do you believe in astrology?*

A: Insofar as astrology can be interpreted, it says something about the life governed by the self-centered nature. Those who follow it become so immersed in the self-centered nature that they do not transcend it.

Q: *When confronted with a problem, can I do anything about it intellectually?*

A: If you are confronted with a health problem, ask yourself: "Have I abused my body?" If you are confronted with a financial problem, ask yourself: "Have I lived within my means?" If you are faced with a psychological problem, ask yourself: "Have I been as loving as God would want me to be?" What you do in the present creates the future, so use the present to create a wonderful future.

Q: *I am troubled much by wrong reactions on my part to what others say and do.*

A: If you really understood everything, all your wrong reactions would turn to compassion. Those who evoke wrong reactions in you are out of harmony, and especially in need of love. Yes, it is most important to be loving. Meet every situation with love, and you will be able to handle it. If someone does the meanest thing to me, I feel the deepest compassion for that person and pray for that person — I do not hurt myself by a wrong reaction of bitterness or anger.

Q: *Is self-discipline really worthwhile?*

A: Perhaps the path toward inner peace does not seem easy while you are walking it, but when you have walked it you look back and think: How could I have earned the great blessing of inner peace so easily?

Q: *What should a person do who is a compulsive eater, and eats wrong foods?*

A: If the person already knows this, and wants to do something about it, the person might begin by having only good, wholesome foods available. Make food a very incidental part of your life by filling your life so full of other meaningful things that you'll hardly have time to think about food.

Q: *How can we dramatize peace?*

A: I think one way to dramatize peace could be through the use of a mobile theater. For a long time I have thought that the arts should be used for the cause of peace. Only a limited number of people will listen to a lecture. More will read all or part of a simple and interesting pamphlet if it is handed to them. Many will listen to the peace people if they can get on radio or television with their peace message. However, just about everybody will look at a drama or a puppet show if it comes right where they are.

Q: *Are we responsible for our thoughts and feelings? Is it fundamentally different from the responsibility for our behavior?*

A: Spiritually speaking, you suffer for negative thoughts and feelings just as you suffer for wrong behavior. However, you suffer most if you know and do not do. Yes, you are responsible for all three.

Q: *What should retirement mean to a person?*

A: Retirement should mean not a cessation of activity, but a change of activity with a more complete giving of your life to service. It should therefore be the most wonderful time of your life: the time when you are most happily and meaningfully busy.

Q: *What should I do when my life seems empty?*

A: If your life seems empty, you have a wonderful opportunity. Most lives are already at least partially filled with not so good things. If your life seems empty, you have a wonderful opportunity to fill it with only good things.

Q: *What should I do when I feel put upon?*

A: Ask yourself whether or not what is required of you is unreasonable. If not, you will attain spiritual growth through serving; if so, you must learn to say 'no' lovingly.

Q: *What overcomes fear?*

A: I would say that religious attitudes overcome fear. If you have a loving attitude toward your fellow human beings, you will not fear them: *'Perfect love casteth out fear.'* An obedient attitude toward God will bring you into the constant awareness of God's presence, and then fear is gone. When you know that you are only wearing the body, which can be destroyed — that you are the reality which activates the body and cannot be destroyed — how can you be afraid?

Q: *How can I conquer little fears, like fear of the dark when alone outside?*
A: I always think of the dark as being friendly. It provides such a restful situation in which to sleep. May I suggest watching it get dark: appreciating the beauty of the sunset and looking for the first star. Get acquainted with the darkness — for fear is usually fear of the unknown.

Q: *Psychiatrists say that all human beings experience fear, but you say that you don't fear anything, not even death. How do you make yourself so totally fearless? Do you have more control over your mind than most people do?*
A: In our early lives we experience as much fear as we have learned in one way or another. Your mind, also your body and your emotions, can only be adequately controlled by the divine nature, not the self-centered nature. If you really love people, you do not fear them. If you live in harmony with divine will, fear is gone. If you identify with that within you which is immortal, you do not fear death. If you fear, it is because your life is still governed by the self-centered nature. Through a great mental effort you may be able to train yourself not to *show* fear — but only when you are governed by the divine nature will you feel no fear.

Q: *What can I do to make my life have more meaning?*
A: Fifteen years before my pilgrimage began, I felt completely willing — without any reservations — to give my life, and I started to live to give, instead of to get. Every morning I thought of God and thought of things I might do that day to be of service to God's children. I looked at every situation I came into to see if there was anything I could do there to be of service. I did as many good things as I could each day — not forgetting the importance of a pleasant word and a cheery smile. I prayed about things that seemed too big for me to handle — and right prayer motivates to right action. My life just blossomed out. Try it.

Q: *How can I begin to really live life?*
A: I began to really live life when I began to look at every situation and think about how I could be of service in that situation. I learned that I shouldn't be pushy about helping, but just willing. Often I could give a helping hand — or perhaps a loving smile or a word of cheer. I learned it is through giving that we receive the worthwhile things of life.

Q: *How can one's life be improved?*
A: Look within for your answers. Your divine nature — your inner light — knows all the answers. Spend your time bringing your life into

harmony with divine law. Work on overcoming evil with good, falsehood with truth, hatred with love. Work on establishing a good lifestyle for yourself. Whether or not you are in the family pattern, these things are important: (1) A means of livelihood which is a useful task in society. (2) Good living habits, including rest and exercise and good eating habits, but most of all good thinking habits — don't think negative thoughts. (3) Inspirational things in your life, things that will lift you up: read beautiful words, listen to beautiful music, experience the beauties of nature. (4) Serve as much as you can, do as much as possible to help others — for in this world you are given as you give.

Q: *How can improving my life help when so many are out of harmony?*

A: Humanity can only improve as people improve. When you have improved your life, you can inspire those around you to want to improve their lives. Remember that a few in harmony with God's will are more powerful than multitudes out of harmony.

Q: *What can a little person like me do for peace?*

A: To the millions who live in this world today let me say that there are many worthwhile things little people can do, both individually and collectively. When I dedicated my life to be of as much service as possible to my fellow human beings someone said to me very sarcastically, "What do you think you can do?" And I replied, "I know I am a little person and can do only little things, but there are so many little things that need to be done." And I never had any trouble finding worthwhile little things to do. When I started my pilgrimage I was asking for very big things and someone said to me then, "You might as well ask for the moon." But I answered, "If enough of us little people ask together even very, very big things will be granted."

I can say this to you: Live the present. Do the things you know need to be done. Do all the good you can each day. The future will unfold.

Poems, Prayers and Songs

Most of the following poems by Peace Pilgrim appeared in a leaflet titled Poems for Our Times. *Her version of* The Beatitudes *appeared in one of her infrequent* Peace Pilgrim's Progress *newsletters and also in* Steps Toward Inner Peace. *Peace enjoyed teaching songs to others, and would frequently end gatherings by having people join in a vigorous and happy rendition of* Fountain of Love.

CHRISTIAN CHURCH

He said, "Of course I may be wrong,
    But I wouldn't be surprised
If this were the greatest Christian church
    That ever man devised.

Our organ is the very best
    Our choir stays on key.
Our stained glass windows — priceless
    Our pulpit — the best you'll see."

But only the wealthy were welcome there,
    I heard slanderous gossip galore,
And from that pulpit so highly prized
    The preacher glorified war.

"Is there anything more you could want in a church?"
    In pride, he said to me.
"Just one thing," I made reply —

    "Christianity!"

WORLD WITHOUT MAN

Before me flowed the gurgling, placid river.
Behind me rose the tree-clad, peaceful mountain.
"Man says this is his world," I reflected,
"And yet there was a time when there was no man.
Did this old world exist the same without him?"
"I was flowing then," murmured the river.
"I was standing firm," whispered the mountain.
"Man now," I thought, "seems bent on self-destruction.
A million fiendish things he has invented —
Each one more deadly than the one before it.
If he succeeds in self-annihilation
Will this world he says is his go on without him?"
"I'll be flowing still," murmured the river.
"I'll be standing firm," whispered the mountain.

WAR FEVER

That terrible blindness —
Which makes your foe appear like a fiend
And makes you look like fiend to him —
    War fever!

That awful insanity —
Which makes the same act brilliant strategy for you
And foul treachery for the enemy —
    War fever!

That frightful drunkenness —
Which muddles the mind until wrong seems like right,
Hate appears good, and murder a virtue —
    War fever!

That horrible sickness —
For which no cure is sought, but instead
Ways are sought to spread the disease —
    War fever!

CONSCRIPTION

In days long past, when men were mere barbarians:
    They chose a man or maybe two, to die
    As sacrifices to the storm god, Thor.

But now that they are civilized and Christians:
    They choose a million men or two to die
    As sacrifices to the stern god, War.

WAR

On the scarred battlefield, where they forced me to go
I met a man that they said was my foe —
    And I ran him through with my blade!

When I pulled it out and his blood gushed forth,
I was suddenly filled with racking remorse —
    "I have killed a man!" I said.

He was slim and youthful and frightened like me,
And not a fiend as they said he would be —
    "They sent me to kill you," he sighed.

"By God! I wish you had done so!" I swore.
"Why, I don't even know what I'm fighting for!"
    "Nor I," he breathed, and died.

THE VICTOR

Amid the destruction created by man
    Nature moves calmly on.
Amid shrieks of the dying and thunder of guns
    Winter has come and gone.

Around the edge of a broken gun
    Tender young grass is showing;
And through the eye of a grinning skull
    A buttercup is growing.

TO A CONSCIENTIOUS OBJECTOR

The Master looked upon the world
    In nineteen seventy-two,
He found men brutalized by hate,
    And few to Him were true,
He saw men shedding human blood —
    Inflicting untold pain.
I heard the Master whispering,
    "To them I spoke in vain!"

But then He spied one gallant man —
    Despised, scorned, and alone,
Because he would not hate and kill
    A prison was his home.
His aim had been, not gaining wealth,
    But serving fellow men.
I heard the Master whispering,
    "In him I live again!"

GREED
(A Story of Men or Nations)

There were two men who had a dispute
    Over a boundary line.
One said, "This land belongs to me!"
    The other said, "It is mine!"

So they fought and fought like two wild beasts,
    And oh, the blood that was shed.
Till one of the men was crippled for life
    And the other man was dead!

Then the cripple lived in misery,
    And he cried in his despair,
"What fools we were so greedy to be!
    There was plenty for both to share!"

YOUR FUTURE

In this world you are given as you give
And you are forgiven as you forgive —
While you go your way
Through each lovely day
You create your future as you live.

PEACE PILGRIM'S BEATITUDES

Blessed are they who give without expecting even thanks in return, for they shall be abundantly rewarded.

Blessed are they who translate every good thing they know into action, for ever higher truths shall be revealed unto them.

Blessed are they who do God's will without asking to see results, for great shall be their recompense.

Blessed are they who love and trust their fellow beings, for they shall reach the good in people and receive a loving response.

Blessed are they who have seen reality, for they know that not the garment of clay but that which activates the garment of clay is real and indestructible.

Blessed are they who see the change we call death as a liberation from the limitations of this earth-life, for they shall rejoice with their loved ones who make the glorious transition.

Blessed are they who after dedicating their lives and thereby receiving a blessing, have the courage and faith to surmount the difficulties of the path ahead, for they shall receive a second blessing.

Blessed are they who advance toward the spiritual path without the selfish motive of seeking inner peace, for they shall find it.

Blessed are they who instead of trying to batter down the gates of the kingdom of heaven approach them humbly and lovingly and purified, for they shall pass right through.

ALOHA OE!

(Peace taught this version of the familiar Hawaiian song to the people who accompanied her on a special inspirational trip to the islands in 1980.)

See this magic land of sparkling waters
And feel the warmth of South Seas sunshine.
As you walk through fields of fragrant flowers
And listen to the sound of sweet Hawaiian music . . .

Aloha O! — My love to you,
Walk gently through this land of sun and flowers.
Aloha O! — God loves you too,
And blesses all your steps along the way!

FOUNTAIN OF LOVE

Fountain of Love
My source is in thee —
Loving thy will
My spirit is free —
Beautiful day
When all of us see
The hope of the world
Is Love!

PRAYER FOR PEACE IN OUR WAR WEARY WORLD

O wonderful spirit of gentleness, touch, calm and embolden us and all men. Take from our frightened hands the bomb and the bayonet. Arm us with faith instead. Arm us with wisdom and love so that wherever we walk in whatsoever land, life will enter and not death. This we know is the will of the Prince of Peace. Amen.

Peace Pilgrim in the News

Peace Pilgrim enjoyed her frequent encounters with newspaper reporters and radio and TV people. She felt the media was a practical and useful way to get her message out to the people of a community. Usually, after the initial professional skepticism, journalists responded positively to her wit, sincerity and willingness to answer their questions thoughtfully.

A Sampling of Headlines:

PEACE PILGRIM TO START HIKE
ACROSS U.S. AS ANTIWAR BID
(Los Angeles Times, January 4, 1953)

'PEACE PILGRIM' IN TOLEDO; SHE'S HIKING 5,000 MILES
Anonymous Woman Plans to Present Pleas to Ike, U.N.
(Toledo Blade, September 17, 1953)

PEACE PILGRIM STOPS IN SEDALIA ON 10,000 MILE HIKE
TO URGE WORLD DISARMAMENT
(The Sedalia, Missouri Democrat, November 7, 1955)

PEACE PILGRIM WALKS FOR PEACEFUL WORLD
(The Clarion-Ledger, Jackson, Miss., January 19, 1956)

PILGRIM'S PROGRESS BRINGS HER TO KENTUCKY
(The Courier-Journal, Louisville, February 27, 1956)

SHE WALKS TO ALERT U.S. TO PEACE NEED
(Bloomington, Indiana, Daily Herald-Telephone, March 8, 1956)

Woman Walks It, Talks It:
REALLY HAS PEACE MOVEMENT AFOOT
(The Indianapolis Star, March 12, 1956)

WITH PEACE HER MISSION, MILES ADD UP FOR PILGRIM
(Northern Arizona University Student Newspaper, Flagstaff, October 4, 1969)

PEACE PILGRIM WALKS 25,000 MILES FOR WORLD PEACE
(St. Louis Post-Dispatch, April 25, 1971)

Little Old Lady in Tennies:
PEACE PILGRIM MARCHES ON ... AND ON ...
(Los Angeles Times, December 3, 1973)

21 Years of Wandering:
PRINCESS OF PEACE WALKS FOR MANKIND
(Pasadena, Calif., Star-News, December 16, 1973)

Energetic Pace Covers 25,000 Miles:
WOMAN ON LIFE-LONG WALKING PILGRIMAGE FOR PEACE
(Pomona, Calif., Progress-Bulletin, February 2, 1974)

PEACE PILGRIM'S GUARDIAN ANGEL WORKS OVERTIME
(Norfolk, Va., Star-Ledger, April 20, 1977)

She Travels Light — a map, her message, a comb,
a folding toothbrush and a ballpoint pen:
MODERN-DAY PILGRIM OF LOVE AND PEACE
(South Jersey Courier Post, Cherry Hill, N.J., October 11, 1977)

PEACE PILGRIM IS STILL WALKING,
BUT SHE'S NOT COUNTING MILES NOW
(Upper Suncoast News, Florida, December 7, 1977)

PILGRIM SET FOR WALK DOWN FLORIDA'S EAST COAST
(St. Petersburg Times, January 5, 1978)

PEACE PILGRIM — A QUARTER CENTURY WALK FOR PEACE
(Whittier, Calif., Daily News, December 30, 1978)

PILGRIM AFFIRMS: MATURITY LEADS TO PEACE
(Colorado Springs Gazette Telegraph, April 28, 1979)

AN AGELESS PILGRIM PURSUES AGE-OLD MISSION
(The Milwaukee Journal, June 22, 1981)

SHE STILL WALKS THE LAND FURTHERING PEACE CAUSE
(Valparaiso, Ind., Post Tribune, July 3, 1981)

PEACE PILGRIM BRINGS MESSAGE OF PEACE TO KNOX
(Starke County Leader, Indiana, July 7, 1981)

Peace Pilgrim to Start Hike Across U.S. as Antiwar Bid

Peace Pilgrim, as she wants to be known until she has completed her mission, plans to leave Los Angeles tomorrow morning on a cross-country hike in the interest of world peace.

"The world situation is grave," she said. "Unless we awake from our lethargy and push firmly and quickly away from chaos, all that we cherish will be destroyed in the holocaust which will descend."

More or less in preparation for her long hike, she walked about 2500 miles last summer, covering the Appalachian Trail from Maine to Georgia and other routes. She learned, she said, how to live outdoors and expects to sleep out most of the time on her trip.

She believes that the way to peace will be found through overcoming evil with good, falsehood with truth and hatred with love. The Golden Rule, she said, would do as well.

Walker WISHING to be known only as the "Peace Pilgrim," this mystery woman will leave Los Angeles today on a cross-country hiking tour to the east coast in the interests of world peace. —(UP Telephoto.)

(Los Angeles Times, January 4, 1953)

171

MESSAGE FOR BOSTON—Describing herself as a "peace pilgrim" but refusing to identify herself this woman talked on Boston Common yesterday and says she has walked 8900 miles in 37 states to promote world peace.

(Boston Herald, July 30, 1956)

(Kansas City Star/Times, Nov. 2, 1955)

WALKING FOR PEACE, a woman who has completed 7,100 miles of an intended 10,000-mile trip arrived yesterday in Kansas City. The woman, who prefers to be known only as Peace Pilgrim, travels without money and depends on the charity of individuals to supply shelter and food. She wears blue slacks, blouse and tunic. The tunic has "Walking 10,000 Miles for World Disarmament" across the back and "Peace Pilgrim" across the front—(Kansas City Star photograph).

172

SHE WHIPPED US—AND HOW WE LIKED IT!

(The Harvey County News, Newton, Kansas, June 25, 1953
Editorial by Floyd Geyman)

Sharing this space with us today is the likeness of a God-touched waif who earned the palm by remaining serene and cheerfully buoyant, in perfect stride, while hurdling all the wiles of a dubious news hound barking on the trail of truth. She licked us — and she left behind some tantalizing thoughts.

She tripped in here, garbed as pictured, and approached the high counter, her face abeam. The first impression was that she was a grease monkey from a service station. But a second glance revealed that the sign emblazoned across her chest, if that's the word, was not the name of an oil company. It was "Peace Pilgrim."

If we would be interested in her mission and her message — here's the story — extending a sheaf of paper, the pages neatly typed. After hasty look-see, one important item seemed to be missing — perhaps an oversight.

"Your name?" with pencil poised.

And that's where the battle of wits began.

"My name is of no consequence," she declared. "I am nothing. My cause is everything. I am not seeking publicity for myself. So far as you are concerned — you and the whole world besides — my name shall remain Peace Pilgrim."

Now there is an old-fashioned idea in newspaper circles that names are news. When you deliberately withhold your name from a news racketeer while seeking publicity in the medium — well, you are doing it the hard way, to say the least. The news sleuth is apt to class you in the same category with the ping who drags in the Fifth Amendment when asked if and when he was born.

"That's a hell of a note," we remarked, stepping into our best religious pose. "Suppose the Christ had assumed your attitude — withheld His name — you never would have heard of Him. Names are tags with which we identify persons and causes and a lot of other things. So kick in if you want any consideration from me — I'm a tough guy, see."

She smiled — and it was not a come-on grin. It was a radiant emanation, natural and serene. With just a touch of imagination, you could see a halo there.

"I'm not afraid," she was saying — not boastingly, but simply, earnestly. "I have the best of protection."

"You mean you carry a thumb-buster — like Calamity Jane," we asked sweetly, "Let's see it."

"God is my shield," she said.

On the Arizona desert one night — she is hot-footing it from Los Angeles to the Atlantic coast, 5,000 weary miles of it, to promote the cause of peace — she saw a car parked beside the way, and a big burly bruiser invited her to climb in and get out of the cold. She did. And it was warm. She curled up in the rear seat and slept the dreamless sleep of the unoffending just. When she awoke, the gorilla told her there was something about it he couldn't understand. He had taken hold of her twice, with evil intent, but he couldn't go through with it.

"What the hell?" he wanted to know.

"God," she told him, and she resumed her walk toward the far Atlantic.

Still mystified, we switched to a brand of strategy that originated in the Garden of Eden, quite a few years ago.

"Let's have your hand," we implored, and she extended her right mitt without the least bit of hesitation. It was a small, firm hand but there was no responding pulsation as we fondled it in the old, old way.

'You have electricity, gal," we lied, in a tone that seldom fails. "Tell me, are you Salome — the dame who danced for the head of John the Baptist, then joined the worshipping throng that followed Jesus to the Cross? Or are you Mary Magdalene?"

But it was no dice — she wouldn't fall for it.

"I'm Peace Pilgrim," she declared.

"Yeah, you're an evil temptress, out to seduce the weak and ruin the world," we informed her, hoping to stir up a spark of anger. "You belong in the hoosgow, and we have a good one here in Newton."

She smiled, and it was not a grin, the kind that shows the teeth rather than reveals the soul.

"I've been in jail," she said. "On vagrancy charges. But they always release me, once they understand."

Now what is one to do with a person like that?

"Have a cigarette?" we invited, extending a beautifully lithographed package. "What kind of whiskey do you prefer — name it and it's yours."

She didn't say "Get behind me, Satan." She said "There's good in you. I really wish I could tell you my name. But it would be unfair to all the other newsmen, radio and television people between here and Los Angeles. You wouldn't want me to do that, would you?"

"Yes," we told her. "Give me your first name, just for a starter —

I'll get the rest of it later on. You've challenged my integrity as a reporter. It simply can't be done."

And do you know, she hesitated, just for a flickering moment. And then she shook her head.

"It wouldn't be fair to the others." And that was that.

We could have told her, of course, that we didn't care two hoots about her name, or the names of all her generations. That we were merely using the tools at hand to sound the depths of her own soul — to see if she was the genuine article or just another phony.

Examining the batch of propaganda, after her departure, we found this written there: "Who am I? Just call me Peace Pilgrim. In undertaking this peace pilgrimage I do not think of myself as an individual, but rather as an embodiment of all human hearts that are pleading for peace."

Well, brethern, sistern, there it is. That's all there is. But somewhere, somewhere, it is recorded that someone, sometime, entertained an angel unaware — and not an angel's underwear, as the little boy read it. Maybe we've had that kind of company. Who knows?

ℐ

Excerpts from Newspaper Stories:

"The group couldn't have been more inspired, stimulated and entertained if the Boston Symphony and the Mormon Tabernacle Choir had shown up in her stead. One might expect an elderly woman clad in navy blue slacks and shirt with matching tunic bearing the words Peace Pilgrim on the front and 25,000 Miles on Foot for Peace on the back to be no more than a quaint, well-meaning eccentric. Nothing could be further from the truth. Plenty of wit, but no nonsense comes from this woman who declines to give her true name, birthplace or date simply because she feels such information 'puts too much emphasis on the person.'

" . . . She mounted the speaker's platform with the briskness of a youthful jogger. With one foot planted firmly on the floor and the other bent forward as if she were about to break into a trot, she spoke for more than an hour, her voice, rich and unfaltering, mass-producing profundities in the simplest and yet most meaningful of terms." (*A California newspaperman*)

" . . . Amidst all technological advancements . . . worries of a nuclear war . . . the USA has today at least one person who sees that the way that pleases the senses, and gratifies worldly desires, does not lead to inward peace. There is a path which requires purification and relinquishment, but results in untold spiritual blessings . . . Peace can be secured only when there is willingness to pay the price. When she explains, it is as though the voice of Gandhi is speaking through her. 'The price of peace is obedience to higher laws . . .'" *(A journalist in India)*

"Her care and guidance comes from Christ — you almost see him by her side. No woman could safely travel alone without a Divine Companion . . ." *('The Wandering Reporter' from Pittsburgh)*

"She has found nothing but interest, assistance and encouragement from the people she has met, and she is convinced that nations, like people, can exist 'on a spiritual level' and that only in that way can real peace come." *(Religion editor, Los Angeles Times)*

" . . . To those of us who sometimes feel the world is slipping into a mire of greed and corruption . . . a visit with this remarkable woman does much to alter the cynic's bitter viewpoint."

" . . . The world has always had soothsayers, seers, self-styled prophets and harbingers of doom, but Peace Pilgrim is different from these because her rhetorical lure, at least, is common sense."

"An Englishman once said to Gandhi, 'Sir you are so simple you baffle us, so sincere you embarrass us.' I would respectfully submit that this statement could also be attributed to a small, aged, yet very vital woman known as Peace Pilgrim."

" . . . A peace phenomenon has been born in the United States and we are blessed for it. A nation that has a war culture and a war economy, that dared to drop the first atomic bomb and has been known to threaten to drop a hydrogen bomb, has produced a lone, silver-haired woman who by her life of walking is saying step after step that there is a better way to live and to solve conflicts . . . By transcending her spiritual humps Peace Pilgrim clarified her mission. She prayed for her pilgrimage and discovered that her pilgrimage was a prayer in itself."

"Meeting a 'Holy Man' is said to be an hourly occurrence in India, and other Oriental countries — but to meet a person in America who is traveling about the land strictly without money in this nation where money is worshipped as it is in no other land, is positively staggering. Yet such a person is now traveling about the state lecturing on world peace — the woman who calls herself Peace Pilgrim . . . She has no fear of anything and has a sunny disposition and is happy to a greater degree than any other person we've met. No mere moneymaker ever attained such peace of mind as is hers.''

"Peace Pilgrim . . . was a woman with a job that extended beyond the realm of what most people could imagine. She was a pilgrim in the truest sense of the word. She touched me in a way that I really didn't understand. She stood very much at ease before a college journalism class in Kansas City, oblivious to the fact that she was being filmed by the *P.M. Magazine* crew. As she began her outspoken method of delivering her message, I wondered at first if she was crazy, or just trying to get publicity for a book that I felt she would surely write about her travels. But as she spoke, something happened to me. She was very sincere with her message. She looked at each student, and made each feel that she was talking to him or her only. Her eyes reached out to each person in the room projecting the love and peace she spoke of . . . There was a strange irony with her being in that classroom. Peace Pilgrim's teachings seemed almost to be out of place in the college environment. After all, college is the stepping stone for America's businessmen and capitalists of the future. Most, if not all, students were present in the school in hopes of getting a good job after graduation, in hopes of making good money. But here was a lady that threw her worldly possessions to the wind, in order to live her life as she saw fit. Why on earth would someone do this? The only answer I came up with is that she truly wanted to do her part in bringing peace to a troubled world. She felt peace had to start with the individual. She kept this philosophy until the day she died.

"The classroom full of college students sat mesmerized in their seats, nearly in disbelief that such a person could survive not only bitter cold nights, but also journeys that took her into some of the roughest neighborhoods in the U.S. To this day it's hard to understand how this 'grandmotherly' type lady could separate herself from a materialistic world, and travel to talk about love and peace.''*(A reporter from Kansas)*

She Walks this World Alone –

Story and Pictures by Richard Polese

She walks alone the breadth and width of America carrying a simple message of peace—peace between men and peace with oneself. She carries with her all she actually owns, she does not accept cash donations and seldom accepts a ride. She will talk anywhere, anytime with anyone who is seriously interested in her pilgrimage. She has been walking and talking in this fashion for more than 13 years.

Last week Peace Pilgrim visited Santa Fe and spoke at a public gathering at La Posada, the College of Santa Fe and St. John's College.

Peace Pilgrim is the only name she now carries. And although her hair is now silver and her face appears scored with the miles of her walk, she speaks brightly, with drama and intelligence and conviction. Her physical fitness is astonishing. She wears a navy blue tunic, with "Peace Pilgrim" lettered on the front, and "25,000 Miles for Peace" on the back (even though she passed the 25,000 mile goal years ago and has since stopped counting the miles).

Why does she call it a pilgrimage? "A pilgrimage involves example and prayer. It can't be called a crusade, which uses at least psychological force." What results does she hope for? "My pilgrimage may at least make people think—to have them question themselves. I leave the results in God's hands."

In her public presentation she talks of the things which are preventing peace; of how a person gains peace within himself, and of her pilgrimage.

Why is there war? "The real problem is immaturity. With real maturity war would be impossible. It would never be considered as a solution of problems between men."

INFORMAL CONVERSATION followed Peace Pilgrim's talk at St. John's College. Surrounded by students at dining hall table, she responded to their questions on the problems of war and peace and her pilgrimage.

But She Walks with the Saints

Finding peace within oneself, Peace Pilgrim says, involves a change in attitude toward life. "It meant living all the good things I believed. It took the living quite a while to catch up with the believing, but it did.

"Simplify your life. There is great feedom in simplicity—more possessions than you actually need burden you...our possessions possess us when we keep them after they are no longer of use to us."

"Purify your thoughts and desires and motives. Hate injures the hater, not the hated. Have a true oneness of desire—just to want to do God's will for you."

"Whether you call it good religious teaching, or sound psychological practices, these things are not new—they are universally valid."

Peace and getting along with others can be made a simple task. "The key is approaching with love and openness, rather than hatred and mistrust —that's what I mean by maturity." Immature people, she says, have negative mind sets, such as a military mind set which sees only military answers.

A religious person, yet not an orthodox Christian, Peace Pilgrim uses a "receptive silence" approach to prayer.

"I'm an optimist because I believe that the laws of the universe work for good—if we obey them. But the choice is ours..." Evidence of her optimism is her expectation that there will be disarmament in her own lifetime.

Peace Pilgrim related that

A LIVELY and colorful speaker, Peace Pilgrim presents her appeal for a peaceful world, and her guide for finding peace within oneself. She is dressed in the lettered tunic she wears as she hikes across the country—a walk which has continued for more than 13 years. Her gray hair contrasts with her remarkable physical vitality. She is shown as she spoke at St. John's College in Santa Fe last week.

(Santa Fe, N. Mex., News, October 13, 1966)

179

Equipped only with a toothbrush, comb and the clothes on her back, this Mystery Lady, who calls herself "the Peace Pilgrim," has traveled 30,000 miles (25,000 of them on foot) across the U.S. and Canada since 1953 on a private mission for peace. She told FAMILY WEEKLY: "I gave up home, possessions, age and name in 1953 because I found them meaningless. I had inner peace—that was all I needed to survive. At the time I felt like a voice crying out in the wilderness, but now I'm definitely on the popular side because most Americans have overwhelmingly accepted the idea of peace.

But world developments have not changed my pilgrimage. Peace is much more than the temporary absence of war; it is the absence of the causes of war. I believe it will take another 10 years for an outer peace to develop and sustain itself, but even after that time I will continue to talk about the inner peace man needs to maintain outer peace." She says her pilgrimage is *not* supported by any group.

MODERN-DAY PILGRIM
She has a mission

Family Weekly Magazine, Dec. 7, 1975

(Continued from previous page)

the new orientation in her life began 28 years ago, with 15 years of "spiritual and psychological preparation" before the pilgrimage began. With no organizational backing, she can be reached only through general delivery in Cologne, N.J.— where a friend forwards her mail to wherever she happens to be at the moment.

When does the pilgrimage end? "The pilgrimage will be over when all nations are like the United States and Canada— where there are still disagreements, but they would never dream of killing each other."

Until that time, Peace Pilgrim will keep walking. She walked down to Albuquerque Saturday following her stay here. And she plans to be back in Santa Fe in 1970. You may see her walking, dressed in her blue lettered tunic, along a highway anywhere in the country. We saw her walking, as a matter of fact, a few years ago somewhere in the Midwest.

A personal pilgrimage

The Topeka Capital-Journal Saturday, November 8, 1980

By PAUL R. JEFFERSON
Capital-Journal religion writer

To hear the Peace Pilgrim tell it, walking all over the United States for almost 30 years in order to spread her gospel of religious faith and personal fidelity is one of the most natural things a person can do.

Wearing a lettered tunic describing her religious odyssey, the self-proclaimed "woman with a mission" continued on her seventh pilgrimage across the country when she passed through Topeka this week.

"I just go wherever I'm invited," said the Peace Pilgrim — her professional name — about her local visits to speak with congregations at the Unity Church of Christianity and the Church of the Brethren. During her week's stay in Topeka, the elderly woman also addressed sociology and psychology classes at Washburn University, and handed out copies of her pamphlet with her "magic formula" for resolving conflicts of all kinds: Have as your objective the resolving of the conflict — not the gaining of advantage.

"Every person is born for a purpose," she said, and added that she gave no mind to being thought "crazy" or "eccentric" by some. Although the Peace Pilgrim was deliberately vague on biographical data, her message shone through her vivid blue eyes.

"You must be living to give instead of to get," she said, "and to promote the causes of peace. Real peace is more than the absence of war; it is an absence of the causes of war."

Beginning her journeys back in 1953, the 70-plus year-old woman has traveled more than 25,000 miles on foot in her east-west, north-south excursions from her home base in Cologne, N.J. Her only accoutrements on her travels, besides the clothes she wears, consist of a comb, toothbrush and a writing pen.

The Peace Pilgrim described her message as one based on God's laws — as outlined in the Bible — and a humanistic mixture of positive thinking and the wealth of human potential.

"All people have potential, but the choice is yours whether you'll finish the physical and mental growth to be able to live up to it," she said. The well-traveled woman added one other aid to reaching one's full potential: spiritual growth.

"As a man thinketh in his heart, so is he," she said, quoting one of many Bible verses which crop up in her public conversations. The Peace Pilgrim has taken her peace-promoting message to schools such as Harvard, Yale, the University of Pennsylvania and University of California-Berkeley, and is on her way to Dallas to lecture at a Catholic convent.

"My seventh peace pilgrimage route will take me through the 48 states in about six years," she said, adding that all of her stops are planned from invitiations she has received.

After first undertaking the cross-country travels on her own, the Peace Pilgrim now receives funding for a newsletter from anonymous donors, but she is not affiliated with any organization or denomination. All of her mail is forwarded from her mailing address in New Jersey.

"I seem like I have lived three lives," she said, in describing how she started her "gentle crusade." After living what she termed "an empty life of money and things" as a young woman, she said she began living a more austere life in the late 1930s, when she began working among the elderly, pared her ifestyle down to a "need level," subsisting on about $10 weekly.

It was then that she took her own intimate vow: "I shall remain a wanderer until mankind has learned the way of peace, walking until I am given shelter and fasting until I am given food." She never carries any money   "I fear nothing and expect good, so good things come to me."

Barney Hubert, Topeka, stopped on US-40 east of Topeka to talk to the Peace Pilgrim when he saw her walking.

Pushing world peace

By Beverly Creamer
Advertiser People Editor

She cuts an eccentrically charming figure — the sneakers, the ponytail, the blue walking suit, each piece a gift from a different friend in a different part of the country.

In the expansive pouch pocket around her middle she has stowed all her possessions — a plastic comb missing a tooth, a collapsible toothbrush, a pen, slips of blue paper that bear her message of world peace, and a bundle of letters from friends all over the country.

"I always wear everything I own," she says, reaching into the pouch and digging around for the letters which she has tucked at the back. On cold nights when she's had to curl up on the edge of a highway somewhere and sleep under the stars — her favorite way to sleep she says, sans sleeping bag — she'll tuck her mail under her blouse to keep her back warm.

For the past 27½ years this woman who calls herself Peace Pilgrim has been criss-crossing America mostly on foot, spreading the message of peace. For the first 10 years she counted miles, she says, and by 1964 had covered 25,000 on foot. She finally couldn't stand counting anymore but kept walking, turning her major attention to informal speaking engagements — at colleges, at truck stops, in churches.

For all of those years she's had no money, won't accept any and hasn't bought a thing — nothing — since she became a wandering pilgrim.

"I was investigated during the McCarthy era to see if I was a vagrant or a religious pilgrim." McCarthy decided she was the latter and let her go. "I'm a deeply religious woman," says Pilgrim. "I'm just not denominational."

In all of that time no one has harmed her. "Of course not," she says, amused by the question. "I live completely on faith." It's never let her down. The longest she's gone without a gift of food is three days.

She hasn't had a doctor's checkup, doesn't worry about getting sick and says she hasn't had an ache or a pain or a headache or a

---

Advertiser photo by Roy Ito

Peace Pilgrim: 'This is what I'm doing with my retirement years.'

— it's a living

in all the years she's been on road even though she's been bed in snowstorms and occally has slept in empty packing s, in parked cars, empty jail , on conference tables, and on the front seat of a fire enin Tombstone, Ariz.

e won't tell you what her origiame was. And she won't tell how old she is, partially bee she's forgotten (although she ts she could figure it out if she y wanted to which she doesn't) partially because she doesn't e to things like birthdays and gages.

: she's got to be 80, says her friend, the Rev. William :z, a pastor of the United ch of Christ in Honolulu. At

9:30 Sunday morning Pilgrim peak at a discussion group at Church of the Crossroads at University Ave. An hour and nutes later she'll speak at the Shepherd Lutheran Church at . Kuakini St. She'll talk about same thing she talks about ever she goes — the golden

es she love everyone she meets? Again the amusement. ourse," she says. "How could l to? Within everyone is a of God. People look to me to hining lights. . . ."

grim says she's seen some ess toward peace in her althree decades of criss-crosser mission, America. "A pils job is to rouse people from apathy and make them " The grey ponytail vibrates e talks. She cuts it herself, by ng it up and hacking off the Keeps it neat, she says.

ere was great apathy when I d my pilgrimage. It was at eight of the Korean War and McCarthy era . . . Just the for a pilgrim to step forth . . . e beginning people thought was a necessary part of life, no alternative. Now they bethere are alternatives possid they're looking for them.

hen I started," she continued, e was no interest in the inner h." Now, she says, "the crisis time has pushed us into inner h . . . I'm still trying to get h . . . I'm still trying to loop e think about their own potenand live according to that

potential."

Pilgrim says it took her 15 years to take the first step, to come to a gradual realization that she needed to give away everything and become a wanderer. She'd been successful financially, she says, and lived in Los Angeles in fine apartments, with fine clothes. But 42½ years ago it started seeming empty, and her friendships started feeling hollow, and she realized there was something else she had to do with her life.

"I never started on my pilgrimage until I found inner peace."

As she says this the weathered brown hands shoot up, fingers pointing skyward. Her wide watery blue eyes sweep to the ceiling and back again. It was then, she says, that she got "plugged into the source of universal energy . . . universal supply . . . and universal truth . . . ."

When she needs new clothes someone always offers them. When she needs food, it is freely given. When she lost a filling once, even that was forthcoming.

Pilgrim does not snow her audience with rhetoric, does not spout book learning in fancy words. Far from it. Her message is simple and contained on slips of blue paper she hands out to all as a kind of quick introduction. Part of it says "Peace Pilgrim's Magic Formula:

"There is a magic formula for resolving conflicts," it reads. "It is this: Have as your objective the resolving of the conflict — not the gaining of advantage . . . " And this: "Be concerned that you do not offend - not that you are not offended."

All of this certainly does not mean Pilgrim is without problems. Far from it. She just looks at them differently. "Problems are opportunities for spiritual growth."

One could say her unorthodox lifestyle probably ensures a full advantage for such growth. Consider this, her second trip to Hawaii. She led an independent educational tour of 15 people on what she calls a two week "camping trip" to the Islands. The airlines don't really like such tours, but they're allowed under Federal Aviation Administration rules and enable her to get a free ticket as tour guide, she says.

"They first tried to tell me to go to a travel agent," she says, smiling a toothy grin. "Well you see," she told them "I can't do that because I'm a wanderer, a pilgrim."

"You're a WHAT?" said the agent.

Pilgrim smiles. "I finally said 'Think of me as a travelling speaker.' They could relate to that."

Pilgrim's little group spent two weeks traveling the islands, sleeping on beaches in parks and cooking over campfires. She ran the tour like she runs her life.

Pilgrim leaves Monday, flying back to Los Angeles and then Bismarck, North Dakota on gift tickets to pick up her pilgrimage course. She alternates between zigzags and loops back and forth across the country, trying to loop through Cologne, N.J. every so often to visit the friend who forwards all her mail. (Her address is Peace Pilgrim, Cologne, N.J. 08213.)

She often gets letters from people who say things like: "'Since talking with you I think I should do something for peace too.' They write their congressman or make peace with a friend . . . It all adds up," she says

Pilgrim corresponds regularly with 10,000 people she's met, sending them irregular newsletters and letting them know when she'll be by. Invariably she's swamped with invitations to spend a night.

"If you fear nothing and expect good, good comes," she says, moving outside to pose for the newspaper photographer. She lies back on the grass, hands tucked under her head in her traditional under-the-stars-warm-nights sleeping pose.

Then she curls forward, arms crossed, hands tucked in armpits, to show how she sleeps on cold nights, explaining "One foot sometimes gets cold if I don't have a map over it."

Finished, she bounces up off the grass and shakes hands. "Money," she says, "I do not accept. I deal with spiritual truth which should never be sold and need never be bought. When you are ready it will be given."

Does she expect others to do what she's done? "Oh no," she says. "This has never inspired anyone else to walk a pilgrimage."

(Colorado Springs Gazette-Telegraph, April 28, 1979)

Pilgrim Affirms:
Maturity Leads to Peace

By JOHN FETLER
GT Religion Editor

She admits that she has something in common with St. Francis in her crusade for peace.

Wherever she speaks, at universities and colleges, in churches, in high schools or on street corners, she gives the impression of having a kind of "inner light" to which young people especially are drawn. Some of them have even asked to become her disciples.

The remarkable thing in an age of gimmicks and cynicism is that nobody seems to take her for a fraud or a charlatan.

Not even for a self-deluded fanatic.

Instead, the silver-haired lady with the startlingly clear-blue and yet serious eyes is taken as just what she is: The Peace Pilgrim.

She was in Colorado Springs for a week. She spoke at a dozen meetings, to as few as five to as many as 500 persons. Then, the early part of this week she took off for Denver to continue her one-woman crusade.

It is her seventh pilgrimage, her seventh crossing of the country.

Before leaving town, she came to talk to the newspaper.

She won't tell her real name, or the years that she has spent in this world, but her appearance is youthfully ageless, her gestures spontaneous with self-evident conviction, her gaze utterly frank. There is vibrancy in her eyes and in her words. She admits to having "tremendous energy." She credits it to her "inner peace."

She was asked: "Haven't things become worse in the world?"

"Oh no," she exclaimed, "just think back a few years ago, to how things were during the Korean War. At that time, war was still the accepted method of dealing with international conflicts. Look at today. Today everybody talks about the necessity for peace. Today war is not acceptable anymore."

The sincerity of her conviction was in her eyes.

But she does not depend on mere enthusiasm.

Even the worst cynic might say: If I don't agree with her about the hope for the future, I can't but agree that she has a logical argument.

She defines the true human being as "God-centered." In this, her conviction is like a rock.

She says she was not raised in any particular denomination, which makes it easy for her to move among all of them. Her record is of delivering seven sermons on one Sunday.

She usually talks in everyday words. But the "religious attitude" does permeate her thinking. It is her firm belief that an individual needs first of all a religious attitude toward God, a religious attitude toward people, and a religious attitude toward oneself.

If she is asked why there is evil in the world, she exclaims "Oh, but that is merely immaturity."

That may not be religious talk, but it is what the psychologists, too, are saying.

How can an individual improve the world?

She says he must find inner peace.

She explains: "Each of us has free will which we can exercise to become mature. I must realize that I am completely responsible for my life. There is no other way."

And that is the reason she refuses to accept "disciples."

"Only God takes disciples," she says. "It is not healthy to follow another human being, only a sign of immaturity. Every person must find his or her own maturity. But it takes time. It took me 15 years to find my own. But the growth period is different for each individual."

"Oh," she exclaims (it seems to be her favorite word, and she says it with that bright cheerfulness that is totally disarming), "I am just trying to inspire people to find what their purpose of life is. No two people are alike. Therefore, no two people have the same job. Each person must find out what his or her job in life is. Then the job becomes easy and joyous."

She says some people have urged her to establish some kind of peace organization of her own, but she has refused.

"I talk to many people in colleges, universities, high schools, in churches," she says. "There is no need of still another organization."

But she regards institutions as essential in achieving world peace.

She explained, "When enough of us mature enough so that we can affect the existing institutions, then things will rapidly change towards peace.

"I accept every human being I meet," she says with disarming simplicity. "I believe that all human beings want to do the right thing, but they don't always know what the right thing is."

As for condemnation or hatreds, she says, "I don't hurt anyone except myself by a negative reaction."

In addition, she receives mail from throughout the country. The Peace Pilgrim's address is simply: Peace Pilgrim, Cologne, N.J. 08213.

"It's just a little farm town," she explained. "A friend of mine agreed to act as a kind of post office box for me. She forwards the mail to me, and I work on the mail in between my talks."

Her project of walking 25,000 miles for peace was achieved in 1964, but she has continued walking for peace as before, with the legend "Peace Pilgrim" stitched on her jacket.

As St. Francis, she is unencumbered by material goods. She is often put up by friends she has won in many parts of the country, she does not accept donations of money.

At first she was a lone pilgrim. Now she is no longer an isolated figure on an American road. She has speaking engagements booked all the way to the beginning of 1984.

Her pilgrimage is being chronicled by Swarthmore College.

PEACE PILGRIM *-Photo by Geoff Appold*

AN INTERVIEW WITH PEACE PILGRIM, JULY 6, 1981

*(Conducted by Ted Hayes, manager of radio station WKVI
in Knox, Indiana, the day before she was killed.)*

Ted Hayes: Peace, let's talk a little bit about this wandering that you have done for peace. How did it all come about?

Peace Pilgrim: Well, it started January 1, 1953 from Los Angeles, California. That year I set out to walk across the country, which I did: zig-zag across 5,000 continuous miles. And then I just continued. I'm on my seventh pilgrimage route now which is my seventh crossing of the country. I have covered the fifty states, the ten Canadian provinces, parts of Mexico. It's an effort to do everything one little person can do for peace.

I walk prayerfully, and as an opportunity to talk with many people and perhaps inspire them to do something for peace also, in their own way.

TH: Peace, what brings you to Knox, specifically?

PP: I was invited to come to Knox by an old friend of mine, Gertrude Ward. I met her elsewhere, so this is my first visit to Knox. And, of course, I do this all the time. It's a part of my regular pilgrimage for peace. I have no money. I don't accept any money. I belong to no organization, so there is no organizational backing behind me. And I own only what I wear and carry. I just walk until given shelter, fast until given food. I don't even ask, it's given without asking. I tell you, people are good. There's a spark of good in everybody, no matter how deeply buried.

Now it used to be that my invitations were just on the spur of the moment. From total strangers I was offered a bed about three-quarters of the time. And I seldom skipped more than three or four meals in a row, but now my invitations often come in advance. And of course that was the case with my invitation to Knox.

TH: Peace, let me ask you this: Was it always Peace Pilgrim, or did you have a name as a little girl?

PP: Oh, it isn't my old name, but if you should address a letter to my old name, I would not even receive the letter. I'm very much Peace Pilgrim now. I am told that it's a professional name, consistently used, you see. It has been my legal name now for some ten or twelve years because, of course, it was taken way back in 1953 when I first started on my pilgrimage.

Things have changed a good deal since then, but I will say one thing has not changed and that is my peace message. It still remains: *This is the way of peace — overcome evil with good, and falsehood with truth, and hatred with love.* That's still the message that I'm carrying after all these years. Well you see, we haven't learned to live it yet. The key word for our times is really *practice.* It isn't more light we need, it's putting into practice what light we already have. When we do that, wonderful things will happen within our lives and within our world.

TH: Peace Pilgrim, you know there are a certain number of people who would not even think of doing this, that would probably think of somebody like yourself as a kook or a nut. Do you have a problem overcoming this barrier with some people?

PP: Well, I'm quite sure that some of those who have just heard of me must think I'm completely off the beam. After all, I am doing something different. And pioneers have always been looked upon as being a bit strange. But you see, I love people, and I see the good in them. And you're apt to reach what you see. The world is like a mirror: if you smile at it, it smiles at you. I love to smile, and so in general, I definitely receive smiles in return. I have been supplied with everything I needed on my pilgrimage without even asking for it.

TH: You walk this country of ours without so much as a penny in your pocket. You just walk on faith alone, faith that somebody will take care of you, and it always seems to happen. You must have some intuition as to whom to approach, whom to smile to, and who is going to be good to you though, don't you?

PP: I smile to everyone. I never approach anyone. I'm wearing my short tunic with *Peace Pilgrim* on the front and *25,000 Miles On Foot for Peace* on the back so folks will stop and talk, and lots of them do. It makes all my contacts for me, in the kindest way. And those who come are very special. They're either genuinely interested in peace or they have a good, lively curiosity. You see, there's a good deal of interest in peace now. When I started out people accepted war as a necessary part of life. And now, of course, we're looking for alternatives to war. It's a gain actually — it's better than it was. When I started out there was very little interest in the inner search. Now there's almost a universal interest in the inner search, which to me is the greatest gain of all. And, of course, since I mostly talk about peace within ourselves as a step toward peace in our world, there is an increasing interest in my subject.

TH: Peace, the Bible tells us that wars will always be with us. What do you say to people who say that? Do you think that this one little effort can make a difference?

PP: It actually says that there will be 'wars and rumors of wars.' But that prophecy has been fulfilled *amply* through the centuries. I don't see why we should want any more fulfillment of that prophecy. It also says 'they shall beat their swords into plowshares and their spears into pruning hooks. Nation shall not lift up sword against nation, neither shall they learn war any more.' Perhaps the time has come for the fulfillment of *that* prophecy. I believe it has.

I think this, of course, is what all of us really desire. And yet, there is so much pessimism. I was talking to a lady who said, "I'm praying with you for peace but of course I don't believe it's possible." I said, "Don't you think peace is in accordance with God's will?" "Oh, yes," she said, "I know it is." I said, "Well how can you tell me that that which is in accordance with God's will is not possible?" It's not only possible, it's inevitable. Only *how soon* is up to us.

Now, I know that all good effort bears good fruit, and so I keep on making what good effort I can. I leave results in God's hands. They may not be manifested in my lifetime but eventually they will be manifested.

TH: Peace, it's not good to, in a regular sense, walk up to a woman you've just met and say "how old are you?" But, I'm going to chance it today. I'm going to ask you how old you are.

PP: I can only tell you that I do not know, and this is deliberate on my part. We create constantly through thought, including we create our age. I had created sufficient age when I started out January 1, 1953, and I said, "that's enough." From that time on I thought of myself as being ageless and in radiant health, and I am. I haven't gotten younger, but I see no point in getting younger. I can get along just fine as I am, and if you have learned the lessons of the seasons of life before, you really have no wish to return to a prior season of life.

TH: Peace Pilgrim has been my guest today. In her literature she says: 'Peace Pilgrim is on my back, 25,000 miles on foot for peace.' And she has finished walking those miles but she continues to walk for her vow is: 'I shall remain a wanderer until mankind has learned the way of peace, walking until I am given shelter and fasting until I am given food.' She appears to be a most happy woman.

PP: I certainly *am* a happy person. Who could know God and not be joyous? I want to wish you all peace.

APPENDIX VI:

Letters to Peace Pilgrim

Following are excerpts from letters written to Peace Pilgrim, mostly toward the end of her last pilgrimage route. Although she forwarded items such as news clippings on to the Swarthmore College Peace Library which collects material about her, Peace followed her vow of simplicity and discarded most letters sent to her after she had answered them.

A friend: "What have you done to me! All I did was ask a nice lady if she wanted a ride, and I end up with a whole new world of wonders before me. Every day now my life is rapidly changing. I simply am not the man I was a month ago, a week ago — yesterday. I continue to find new meaning in our conversation."

A friend: "When I opened your letters, my soul was in turmoil, with my lower self doing battle with my higher self — and winning, I'm afraid! Your wonderful messages washed over me like a bath, cleansing and purifying! What you say makes so much sense — TRUTH, all in capital letters!"

A college professor: "Perhaps you'd like to know, final exam Philosophy 201 tomorrow will consist of quotes from and questions about your aphorisms."

A correspondent: "I have heard William Jennings Bryan, the greatest orator of his generation. I also heard Dr. Russell Conwell give his famous lecture, *Acres of Diamonds,* and I want to say at this time the lecture you gave was superior to Bryan's effort or the genius of Conwell."

A friend: "Thank you so much for sending the literature. I find it all very profound. It strikes a chord in me that keeps resounding . . . Your correspondence to me arrived like an answer to a prayer — it came on a day of enormous need for inner peace, and the tangles seemed to melt away. It was very comforting."

A minister in Texas: " . . . I gave your booklet, Steps Toward Inner Peace to the East Coast ministers. They all would love to have you speak at their churches. I told them you were the best thing that ever happened to our church — and I meant that sincerely. I know you are a blessing to this whole world."

A friend in Baton Rouge: " . . . I sincerely hope your sane and life-giving message of peace is finding receptive audiences wherever you travel . . . Many are becoming more and more concerned with the shocking and outrageous militarism which we now hear preached on every hand. Surely no individual of conscience can support or justify such massive preparations for the wholesale destruction of the human family. How truly wonderful it would be to see the final triumph of peace and justice over the forces of death and destruction . . . "

Catholic Sister from California: "For some good reason you keep crossing paths with Catholics working for peace . . . You are a *today witness to Jesus' peace.*"

A college student in Illinois: "It's been a few months since I met you . . . and your message has been on my mind since that time. I've listened for so long to 'successful people' tell me what life was all about and I followed their advice blindly. However I found what I had been seeking in a small white-haired lady with no possessions . . . "

A minister: "Thank you for your inspiration and encouragement. You were a 'God Send' to our congregation. Our church is experiencing new life, harmony and mission outreach."

A college student: "Since hearing your message I have done a lot of self-evaluation and reorganization of the values and priorities in my life. I discovered a person within me with an overwhelming desire to reach out and share with others who had been buried beneath self-interest and fear. I have been so busy trying to survive and possibly get ahead that I missed out on a lot of the living. I had been waiting for someone to open up an escape hatch in the wall of apathy and disillusion that surrounded me. The message of hope and love that you shared with our class that night helped me to open up and to see that there was a lot of good left in our world. There are so many out there like myself who are waiting for someone, anyone, who cares to come along and touch them . . . While I may never have the courage to travel as you do, I can reach out to those persons in Springfield . . . I want to thank you for *helping me to believe in people* — with all of this education it was one thing I never learned . . . Your commitment to peace and love radiates from your face, there is no need for you to persuade or debate the issue . . . God truly blessed you . . . May your light shine for many more years."

A friend: " . . . meeting you has meant a lot to me. For the first time I have wondered what my role in the divine plan is — it never occurred to me before that there could be something special I should be doing . . . "

A radio listener: "In 51 years of listening, reading and discussion, I have never heard nor seen the truth — as it relates to both inner and outer problems so beautifully and logically promulgated as by you on the local radio program today — You have a tremendous grasp of the problems that are plaguing people and governments today; and the solutions you speak of seem so logical and full of promise."

Letters About Peace Pilgrim

People who met Peace wrote not only to her, but also to their friends, relatives, ministers, and newspaper editors. Many felt compelled to share the news of their encounter with others and urged them to find where she would be speaking when she came through their town.

A radio listener: "I can't remember when I have been as interested and inspired by a person speaking about their inner peace and joy as I was last evening, hearing the interview with that splendid human being, the Peace Pilgrim . . . Her undogmatic and selfless faith has affected me after one listening more than all the sermons, masses, rules, philosophies, etc., I have ever heard in my life."

The couple who gave Peace Pilgrim hospitality on the first night of her pilgrimage, January 1, 1953: "Indeed we were really excited to meet someone who was willing to live as Christ did. Her message is one of love and love is the healing force, so what she says is certainly what the world needs."

A minister: "Peace's faith in God and humanity is beautiful to observe. She has as perfect a balance between the personal and social gospel as anyone I know."

A college professor: "I first met Peace Pilgrim five years ago when she spoke before my classes. It was such a moving experience for all of us —to be in the presence of someone who was truly living her beliefs and faith. This year when Peace Pilgrim returned to Los Angeles she again met with my classes. If anything her message was even more illuminating and inspirational. I have never heard anyone express in a more beautiful and challenging way what it means to be a human being. And what is possible for each of us as a human being. Her life is a living testimony to the truth of her message."

A friend: "Peace Pilgrim is either an eccentric old fool or an authentic prophet! The choice is ours to make when we meet her. But what is most extraordinary is that she is neither offended by the former description or esteemed by the latter. If Peace is a fool, she hides her foolishness well; if she is a prophet, a mist of humility equally hides her greatness. She is a fathomless enigma. One must continually pinch her here and pinch her there in a determined effort to see if she is for real."

A minister: "A crackpot? A peculiar person? Strange to talk to? Not at all. She has more common sense than anyone I have ever met."

Observer at a lecture: "When the Peace Pilgrim talks everyone sits spellbound. Her words are simple but lofty, her way loftier still. But she has by no means lost the common touch and this endears her to all present. She is not advocating we drop everything and become pilgrims like herself nor is she a fanatic prophesying doom."

A letter to an editor: "The Peace Pilgrim, who visited our town for two days, has come and gone. Are we not haunted some as we reflect upon her presence? Are we not left recalling one who walked the road of Galilee two thousand years ago; who denied himself . . . family and those things which we usually identify with success, who had no place to lay his head, but undertook all to tell the story of salvation and hope — the one whom we now call the Prince of Peace?

"We may be grateful that it can be hardly said of our town what was said of certain towns where Jesus stopped. There is no needed assumption to shake the dust of our town off her feet by being refused a hearing . . . She was given a warm reception.

"Surely the Peace Pilgrim's presence does hauntingly sensitize us to the truth revealed by her spirit. Certainly we all know we stand on the knife-edge between a war of annihilation and a golden age of peace . . . We may not all walk the pilgrim's journey with vow of poverty, on foot and on faith. But the presence of the Peace Pilgrim may well call to each of us to reflect on what we are doing for the cause of peace."

A friend: "At a time in my life when I was wrestling with the possibility of idealism in principles and actions, I found myself searching out individuals whose teachings and writings appeared exemplary. Every opportunity to observe such an individual was approached in high expectations. Without exception I can say that every experience of this sort was leading me to the conclusion that idealism was a state of mind.

An almost magnetic attraction pulled me towards the pursuit of idealism in daily life, yet the lack of a living archetype left me discouraged. It seemed that all the idealists were characters of literature. Then, through the workings of fate, I was led to an encounter with a master soul, a woman whose name long ago became Peace Pilgrim.''

An Iowa Minister: ''We have just experienced a weekend with Peace Pilgrim, and we would recommend that people not only hear her but spend some time discussing her philosophy with her. She seems to be equally adaptable to many different kinds of situations.

''She spoke in our two morning worship services and at an evening lecture — to unusually large audiences, due partly to advance publicity through newspaper, radio and television. She spent time with two smaller groups, and spoke twice at a two-day, statewide interdenominational ministers' retreat. She was equally at home at an 80-minute convocation of students, professors and townspeople on the Morningside College campus; and commanded attention and respect at a dinner meeting, with college professors and administrative personnel for an hour and a half.''

A California minister: ''She made the greatest single impression on me and my life . . . Her talk (on attaining inner peace) was the finest metaphysical message I have ever heard. She is a pillar of strength, when strength is so needed. She is a radiant light, when light is so needed. She actually reflects the qualities we say are Christlike. I — along with many of the others who heard her — felt reinforced and indeed blessed.''

A minister in Kentucky: ''To hear Peace tell of the spiritual experience that motivated her work is truly a moving spiritual experience for the listener. You will never be privileged to meet a happier or more loving person than Peace, because she lives in the presence of God and her every word and movement express her conscious awareness of the One Presence and the One Power.''

A minister in Houston: ''The direct simplicity of this modern saint is not only refreshing, but also a clear channel of constructive action for our times . . .''

A friend in Colorado: ''I met her as an answer to a wish in about 1968 . . . She was on television being her own beautiful self. I thought, ''I wish I could meet you, I need to talk to you.'' So, the next morning as I was getting on the freeway, here stood Peace at the entry needing a ride. That car of mine came to a sudden halt and I said, ''Get in here, I've been waiting for you.'' I kept driving for three hours toward Nashville where she was to speak . . . It was one of the most wonderful visits of my life. I talked to her about writing a book.''

Radio station manager in Maryland: ''I have today had the pleasure to interview one of the most unusual persons I have ever met — Peace Pilgrim.

''She is a literate woman of great talents and conviction and is a very stimulating speaker. Without propounding any foolish ideologies or rubbing anyone the wrong way, she brings a message which is of interest and concern to everyone.''

A hostess who arranged speaking opportunities: ''Peace Pilgrim was by again. About 24 years ago we met this remarkable woman, living a life of peace and harmony unequaled by anyone we've ever known. Through the years she has visited in our home when she was passing by. She has been a continual and growing inspiration in our lives . . . The really glorious thing, of course, is seeing and knowing a real person through the years, full of endless energy and hearing her say it is there for all of us.''

◊

Following her death in July 1981, letters continued to pour into the little post office in Cologne, New Jersey — often from people who did not know who they were writing to, but who wanted to share with others who were close to Peace Pilgrim. Many wrote poignant and eloquent expressions of how they were moved by her visits, her life and her message.

A minister in Dallas: ''There was just no one like her. She made a contribution to this world of ours, which is absolutely unique. Her singleness of purpose, her dedication and her love, humor, warmth and high consciousness changed the lives of many of us . . . ''

A friend in San Diego: ''Her presence always inspired me and I went to as many of her meetings in my area as I could, never tiring of hearing her message over and over . . . It was her influence which decided for me to come to California in order to live more simply and not earn enough to have to pay taxes to support war. I try not to have anything I don't really need. There is no way to know what influence she may have had on the growing, little publicized movement for a transformed world; I sense it may be considerable . . . She inspired us to live what we believe and act on it to the best of our ability and to then leave the results in God's hands . . . ''

An American Red Cross Employee: "I first met Peace in the early '60s when I was at the University of Wisconsin. Peace came into town. A small, somewhat loose group marched from campus to the capitol with Peace at the head . . . those marches later became huge . . . but one of the first in modern times was led by Peace.''

A college professor: "Peace Pilgrim visited our campus by invitation. She spoke to classes in psychology, sociology, philosophy and religion as well as to a general assembly of students and faculty. She was enthusiastically received.''

A Catholic nun in South Dakota: "Peace Pilgrim made such a difference in my life! It is impossible to describe how she affected me. Also she had a tremendous impact on the student body here at the college. Her gentle kindness will live forever in my heart.''

In a newssheet from Texas: " . . . She literally brought 'heaven' onto earth. She brought the divine qualities into her life here . . . She changed lives all over America . . . ''

A friend in Maryland: "Peace was indeed a light and a living example of truly Christlike living to many thousands of people . . . How privileged I have felt over the years to be in close contact with such a radiant, loving and giving teacher and friend.''

A friend: "I followed her for weeks in Hawaii . . . sleeping on the ground. Mosquitoes were so bad, at one time I was on my third spraying trying to get to sleep, she was sound asleep, not one touched her and she never used anything to stop them. I felt she had truly achieved at-onement with all the elements and living things . . . ''

A minister in Indiana: "Her memory and work are fresh in many minds, but memory is short, and the passage of time causes us to forget that which we think we will always remember. It is natural that writers will want to capture her spirit in books and that documentaries will be thought of. Hers was a full and free spirit, and that will not be easy to capture . . . Her life was her message and it is almost impossible to capture that in a written passage . . . ''

A minister in Indiana: "... how much better place this world is for her having travelled this way ... she in her way, and with her particular talents, reminded us that we too will be blessed as we work for peace, both within ourselves and in the world community ..."

Another Indiana minister: "Peace Pilgrim left a profound effect over the entire nation in personal lives touched by her radiant and committed spirit. Thanks be to God that she walked amongst us ..."

A friend: "I believe that each of us should be given, at some time in our lives, the wonderful privilege of meeting a saint. Having spent some time with Peace Pilgrim I believe I've had that honor, for to me Peace Pilgrim is a true saint."

A friend: "She was one of the most remarkable women of our century ..."

An editor for a metropolitan newspaper in Dallas: "Love was her path, her shield, her weapon and her all. Some thought she was crazy but she loved them nonetheless. 'I sure would like to write a book about you,' I said to Peace Pilgrim the last time I visited with her ...

"We know Peace Pilgrim is liberated. We know her work will continue. I am glad I got to know her and finally understand her and accept her lifestyle."

A woman who was expecting Peace Pilgrim to come to her home in Ann Arbor: "Whenever I hear ... songs of peace, and as we continue to work for a more peaceful world, it will be with an awareness of that special person whose life touched ours briefly, but whose influence has been profound wherever she went."

A friend in Portland, Oregon: "Her death is a loss not only to us who have known her but also to the entire world ... We all loved Peace Pilgrim ... she changed our lives for the better ... we know that she is continuing her high mission for humanity."

An editor for a publishing house: "I have the feeling there is more Peace Pilgrim in the world than before. That she is closer than I've ever known her. Each of us now has a part of her ... *is* a part of her, and she is a part of us ... I join with you in a circle of love, with all the others who know her and were touched by her. We have work to do!"

A young man in West Virginia: "I met Peace Pilgrim when I was a senior in college in 1973. She was a guest speaker in a psychology class [to discuss] psychological growth. I found her to be very inspiring and attended other classes and meetings on campus where she spoke. Over the years, I would think of her and her messages from time to time. Those remembrances always lifted my spirits.

"After graduating I worked for three years with neglected, abused and delinquent youth in a non-secure facility. We . . .found alternatives to incarceration for hundreds of children and were committed to dealing with difficult children without the threat of or use of physical punishment or detainment.

"I am now working towards my Masters degree in social work, pursuing a 'Peace Studies' concentration . . . with six month internship at the Draft Information and Referral Center, counseling about registration and draft options, including conscientious objection and war resistance . . . I have helped form a 'Peace Studies Club' in the local high school and a 'Center for Peace Studies' at the university.

"I have reduced my number of possessions so that I can store them in a locker on campus where I change clothes and shower. I keep a sleeping bag on a friend's porch and sleep in a nearby woods, finding shelter in the park when it rains.

"After my internship ends this fall, I plan to work at several part-time jobs, hopefully earning about $200 a week. I will donate all of the $200 to a needy organization that is working for peace, social justice, or environmental improvement. For every ten dollars that I give, I will ask for a one dollar matching donation to be given to myself. Thus, if I give $10,000 a year, I will receive $1,000 from various individuals, which I will be able to live on.

"Peace Pilgrim was scheduled to come to West Virginia again next Spring. I know that there were many groups and individuals that were looking forward to seeing her. I was hoping to discuss my plans and ideas with her. However, I feel grateful to have met her once. Studying people like Mohandas Gandhi, Martin Luther King, Leo Tolstoy, Albert Einstein, Dorothy Day and others has inspired me and deepened my faith in non-violence . . . Peace Pilgrim has meant more to me than those people, and is partly responsible for my choosing the work with youth, the peace studies curriculum, and especially my more recent plans. Since the eight years when I met her, her words have been a source of comfort and inspiration to me. I can still remember her talks vividly.

"Peace has helped me to pay attention to the voice within me that I might have otherwise ignored as being foolish or impractical.

"I hope in this letter that I have been able to adequately express my thankfulness for knowing Peace and her message, and how deeply I believe that she has touched my life."

A couple in California: "Peace Pilgrim has strengthened our faith in the reality of the spiritual world and has given us a concrete example of something we never dreamed possible: a person filled with inner peace and boundless energy that grew with time. She has given us hope of finding that same universal energy because she insists that it is there for all of us. 'If I can find it, you can too,' she would say. The greatest inspiration of all is that her life and her words were one. She was her message."

APPENDIX VIII:

Experiences with Peace Pilgrim

The following letters are from people who had the opportunity to spend some time with Peace Pilgrim.

A friend who met Peace Pilgrim before her pilgrimage: "Not long before Peace Pilgrim made her debut ahead of the Pasadena Rose Parade [January, 1953], a friend escorted a woman walking barefoot and carrying her shoes, having come from the beach. She wore shorts and an abbreviated blouse. Soon after my husband and I had been introduced to her, our conversation became so interesting that I phoned three friends and persuaded them to hurry over and meet her. We all enjoyed supper together, after which we joined the village folk-dance group — followed by conversation back home which continued into the early morning hours.

"She spoke of her work in Washington, D.C., where she served as a legislative lobbyist for a peace group. (About ten years later, I attended a National Legislative Seminar in Washington, held by the Woman's International League for Peace and Freedom. I learned that she had been their peace lobbyist and that she had without a doubt been the most effective one they had ever had.) She told us that the longer she worked with Congressmen, the more convinced she became that the road which these men were persisting on following could only result in eventual war. As this conviction grew, she began to be consumed by a gnawing question. As she put it, 'I am not afraid for myself. But if a debacle occurs, what group will preserve for humanity the best in our culture? The monasteries served us well in this regard during the Dark Ages. What group is adequately structured to do it this time around?'

"She realized she could never learn that answer by remaining in Washington; and since nobody else seemed concerned about this aspect, she felt driven to quit her job and try to find it herself. For over a year she had been hitch-hiking across the country, visiting every group she could find which was dedicating itself to the task of formulating workable group living patterns that were based on love and sharing.

"'After all my searching,' I recall her saying, 'I decided that I'd found one coming close to meeting the need of preserving our culture during the difficult years that lie ahead — Koinonia Partners, in Georgia. But not even it comprises the complete answer.'

"When at last we said goodbye, all of us were aware of her deep longing to find answers that would enable her to contribute usefully to the task of ushering in a world based on love and cooperation between nations. It could not have been many months later when we learned that at last our remarkable friend had found her proper niche in our rapidly changing world and would henceforth serve us all in her special way.

"Three years later we were living in San Bernardino, California, when we learned that soon Peace Pilgrim would be passing through. She accepted my offer to schedule her appearances during her stay in our city. A Methodist minister arranged for her to appear at a church dinner, and we worked out a full calendar. I booked her for our YMCA Creative Living Club, a health study group. Our president and half of our members were Seventh-Day Adventists. He came to an earlier meeting to size her up, since many of them wondered, 'what did he know about this strange woman he was bringing to speak to us?' Later he told me, 'Peace Pilgrim is just wonderful! *WONDERFUL!* I've never seen anyone like her! And that bunch of doubting Thomases will all love her too. She is going to be the best speaker we have had.'

"The morning of Peace's arrival the minister instructed me that if she called from an outlying area, he would run right out and pick her up. When she called, I relayed the offer. She refused emphatically, stating that very important contacts came as she walked through the outskirts of a city. A couple of days later we learned what she meant. Strangers kept coming to our meeting at the Y, and a second time we had to move into a larger room. Almost all these newcomers arrived as the result of her gracious invitation while talking to them on her way in.

"Before turning Peace over to her hostess, I handed her the updated schedule of her speaking engagements with churches and civic groups. After looking it over, she asked if we had a college in our town. A moment later she was on the phone persuading the journalism professor at the University of California at Riverside that it would sharpen the skills of his students if he permitted them to interview her. Heavy as her schedule already was, she squeezed this in. What an organizer!"

Another friend who knew Peace Pilgrim before her pilgrimage: "I met Peace Pilgrim some time after World War II, when I was teaching in Philadelphia and doing volunteer work in the Fellowship of Reconciliation office almost every afternoon. She was then using a small partitioned part of our office to take care of the publication and distribution of Scott Nearing's *World Events*, which I think came out bimonthly, as well as doing miscellaneous volunteer work for the Womens International League for Peace and Freedom. She was very quiet and efficient in the job. When it was time to mail *World Events*, she assembled a group of interested people who did the folding and addressing in one evening. She took $10 a week for her living expenses, which she explained, was more than ample.

"I think at that time she owned two dresses, which she wore alternately. She always looked very neat, sober, fresh and trim like a sparrow, and in fact there was something sparrow-like in her constant cheerfulness, her bright eyes, and her liveliness. She belonged to a hiking club which went on frequent long trips and once a year, I think, had an endurance hike of forty miles or so. She was a little complacent about always finishing the hike, though most of the members dropped out after thirty miles.

"She went to the West Coast, hitch hiking in her fearless way, and spent about two years, I think, working in several health institutions and thinking about the methods. She was most impressed by Shelton in Texas who used fasting as his only treatment.

"My only criticism of her work (if it is a criticism) is that to most of her hearers she was offering 'peace of mind' — a commodity very much in demand in the modern world and nowhere so much as in the U.S. I know that she never failed to bring world peace into her message, but I feel that it was often obscured by the personal needs of the people who heard her. But she brought the message to tens of thousands of people whom the peace movement cannot touch."

A friend who took Peace Pilgrim to Alaska and Hawaii to meet his relatives: "I remember once in our early acquaintance I posed a question to Peace: 'Sometime in your wanderings you must have been walking down a country road and run smackdab into a motorcycle gang who terrorized communities.' I remember her looking up at me and responding, 'Leon, you don't understand.' To which my response was, 'Well, I certainly understand such a condition.' I remember her placing her hand on my arm to get full attention and stating it this way, 'No, Leon, you do not understand. You see, I go where they are; I do not ask them to go where I am.' I pondered over this response for a long time. It was not until several years later that I had an insight into her meaning.

[In Hawaii they met a young man in a park on the Big Island.] "He asked about Peace and myself. We told him we had just entered the park and did not know where we were or how to get where we wanted to go. He asked

to be our guide to show us unusual and exciting things of which he was aware in the area. Peace accepted this offer and we followed him around the park for the next hour or more.

"I don't know that I can describe the personality of this young man with acuity. He was somewhat 'beered' up, I am sure. He was totally unrestricted in buoyant, loud, enthusiastic expressions that were ongoing. He was 'hyper' in his mannerisms and in his enthusiastic efforts to show us his domain. His every sentence was filled with four-letter expletives of the crudest kind. He was totally unaffected in his demeanor. To say the least, I was embarrassed to be in the company of such a person. It was not long until we were at the visitor center, which was crowded with tourists in their colorful island garb, milling around. The air was festive. My humiliation in being in company with this boisterous young man was extreme. What could Peace be thinking of to allow this, was an enigma to me. In short, I suffered.

"It was not long thereafter that we found ourselves out at the brink of the live volcano cauldron, standing on the observation platform. Our time had run out. We must start back to Hilo to meet the schedule for our returning plane. Peace turned to the young man, thanked him for his help and told him it was time for us to leave. There was no question about his disappointment and reluctance to see us leave. He stood there, with tears running down his cheeks and dropping from his chin, begging us to let him show one more special area that he knew about.

"As I stood there looking into the face of this young man, I was reminded of Peace's words several years before: 'I go where they are. I do not ask them to come where I am.' The condemnation that I felt for myself was extreme. Still I knew at that moment an admiration and humility that was also overpowering. As I grapple to set aside the demands of an ego-centered life expression and enter into the fullness of a God-centered life, I have often looked back on this personal experience with Peace when she gave me by example an awareness that I treasure so highly."

From Mary O'Kelley, a friend of both Peace Pilgrim and Congresswoman Jeanette Rankin, the only U.S. Representative to vote against both world wars (Jeanette had phoned Mary that she wanted to meet Peace Pilgrim):

"We finally got together and planned for Peace Pilgrim to spend the night with her, and she would invite some people in to meet Peace Pilgrim and hear about her pilgrimage. After the plans were made Jeanette turned to me and said, 'Whom shall I invite?' Then I discovered she lived there alone. No friends! No neighbors!

"Jeanette had bought land in the county when she was in Congress. She had lots of friends in Athens [Georgia]. When she voted against the entrance into World War I the people were not very pleased. When she was in Congress again in 1941 and voted against war again, that was too much, so they burned her house down. She had land a little nearer the center of the county so she moved into a little house. This was twenty years later — but she still felt the sting. She was bitter — felt that no one liked her, felt the men in Congress were heading us down a bloody trail to destruction.

"I suggested that she telephone the neighbors. Some of us from Athens came, and it was a packed house. I think she had between 50-60 people.

"After the meeting, Peace and Jeanette spent the night talking. Jeanette was thrilled that the people came, and Peace saw a real need for Jeanette to get active in living, that her bitterness was eating her up. Jeanette asked what she could do. Peace told her that with her name she could do a lot, and with her finances she could do even more.

"Peace said she talked rather firmly about the need and her debt to society. She said she felt that Jeanette was seriously considering getting involved. In the spring there was an organization formed on the university campus — a feminist group. Jeanette became involved.

"She was a lovely lady. Peace showed her how to start her road back to the 'family of man.' Slowly she began to change. She picked up where she had left off in the forties. She led the national group that went to Washington [the Jeanette Rankin brigade during the Vietnam War]. She spent the rest of her life working on women's rights."

A Franciscan Sister: "In the 70's Sister Johnella saw Peace Pilgrim on TV and became pen pals with her, but she had to wait six long years before meeting her. Sister Driver brought her to our Villa home, and what a warm welcome she received! Everyone wanted to say something to her. Sister Johnella was beaming all over and couldn't get away from Peace Pilgrim. She gave us a talk with prayer in the Community room.

"Three years later she came for three days and two nights. She felt quite at home and loved our beautiful park-like grounds. She spoke in the mornings to those of us who had no pressing duties and also in the afternoons and evenings. Her charm, warmth and sincerity had attracted us to her.

"One morning we washed her personal things, and she took a warm bath. We told her we would gladly supply her with new shoes and tunic, but she said she preferred we did not.

"One day, I had more time to visit her by myself and we got well acquainted. I said to her, 'I would like to be a companion to you and do the same things together for peace, to keep you company so you would not be alone.' 'No,' she said, 'you cannot help me or come with me, as much as I would like to have you. It is a mission very different and only for one person, me, Peace Pilgrim.' Then she said to me, 'When my mission of Peace ends and I am gone then Peace will come.' She was a prophet; peace is now coming. She talked of her early experiences on highways and in cities, how God had always protected her."

A TV talk show host: "The Vietnam War was raging. I had just begun doing a TV talk show for WSM in Nashville. Being fresh and without much maturity . . . and eager to make an impression, I relished the thought of this 'kook' being on . . . I personally booked her, after reading her letter to me that she was headed (walking) in this direction. When she entered the TV studio, I laughed along with the audience, the band and the crew. Who is this grandma hippie?

"I presented her with all the brashness and ill-taste that I could muster. In those days, making fun of 'peace people,' especially in the good ol' boy region of the country, got reaction. The first few minutes of the interview she bantered with me — sparred, perhaps is the right term. She was neither defensive nor aggressive. But, oh those eyes . . . and those hands . . . reaching, groping at some invisible point in the air to make her point . . . and those sparkling blue eyes. After perhaps two, maybe three minutes, I was in the palm of her hand. I felt embarrassed, shameful. She seemed to sense it, and I felt as if she had seen through the game all along and knew the moment of realization lay within the interview.

"When the eight minutes were over, there were only a few snickers from the audience, none from the band. The radio show that followed, one hour, was straight ahead, no bad jokes. I grew up a lot that day . . . . There were other interviews with her in the years to follow, but none as memorable as the first."

*Peace Pilgrim
as a young woman.*

Photograph by Jim Morrill, courtesy Linda Ann Scott

FRIENDS OF PEACE PILGRIM

At this writing, it has been nine years since Peace Pilgrim made what she would have called her "glorious transition" after 28 years on pilgrimage. Her inspiring peace message continues to be spread in ever-widening circles. This book and her little spiritual classic, *Steps Toward Inner Peace*, are now found in more than 100 countries. The *Peace Pilgrim* book, published a year after her death, is in its thirteenth printing with 200,000 copies now in print.

The *Steps* booklet, compiled and distributed while she was living, has been translated into Spanish, Russian, French, German, Serbo-Croatian, Polish, Tamil, Chinese, Norwegian, Swedish, and Danish, and had appeared in print in the first five of these languages.

In the spirit of Peace Pilgrim, who gave her time and energy freely, the five compilers of the *Peace Pilgrim* book decided to try to give a free book to anyone who asks. They agreed to continue this policy as long as enough unsolicited donations were received to reprint. And inspired readers have contributed enough for many books to be sent to prisoners, to the unemployed, to those working for good causes for low wages or as volunteers, to people in third world and Communist countries, and to others who cannot send gifts.

Friends of Peace Pilgrim is a non-profit, tax-exempt organization with an all volunteer staff. At this writing there are four full time volunteers, including two of the compilers of this book whose home is now the Peace Pilgrim Center. In addition, numerous people help out on a part time basis. Last year, Friends of Peace Pilgrim sent out over 35,000 copies of this book, and over 4,000 audio cassettes and 1,000 video cassettes of Peace Pilgrim's public talks and question and answer sessions.

Friends of Peace Pilgrim also provides Spanish and Russian language editions of Peace Pilgrim works. *Steps Towards Inner Peace* is now available in both of these languages. Russian and Spanish editions of this book are in preparation and will be available soon.

For a list of free offerings write to:

Friends of Peace Pilgrim

Telephone (909) 927-7678
43480 Cedar Avenue, Hemet, CA 92544
Telephone: (714) 927-7678